Worlds Apart

Jenni Shell

Maat Publications
www.orderofthewhitelion.com

Cover drawing: Authors father, aged 2 years
Geoffrey Turner (1909 – 1987)
Artist - Leslie Austin

Published by Maat Publications

Production and Design: Drew Westcott
www.drewwestcott.co.uk

ISBN: 1500763519
ISBN-13: 978-1500763510

To my dear mother and Sandy
Who knew each other once

"I am an orphan, alone: nevertheless I am found everywhere. I am one, but opposed to myself. I am youth and old age at one and the same time.

I have known neither father nor mother, because I have had to be fetched out of the deep like a fish, or fell like a white stone from heaven.

In woods and mountains I roam, but I am hidden in the innermost soul of man. I am mortal for everyone, yet I am not touched by the cycle of aeons"
Carl Jung.

CONTENTS

Table of Contents

Acknowledgments

With many thanks to Marius and Mike, for their advice and support whilst writing this book: and to Drew for helping to make it happen.

A THOUGHT

"Real knowledge is to know the extent of one's ignorance"
Confucius

This is a twofold story – my mother's and mine - for it was her life and her terrible burden that became my care, my quest, and my deep unending pain, in the search for a reason that would help explain her illness.

And through it all I discovered many things, including realities that may not seem to exist here on earth - but actually do exist, although often remain elusive in our world of understanding.

Sometimes we can't see what is real, for it is not "reality" in the normal sense of the word. But, in spite of how it may seem sometimes, we do control and direct the course of our lives   - whether we are conscious of this or not.

Whilst reading this book, you may feel you wish to participate, by examining your own impression of the very personal world you have built for yourself: and how your focus and determination – or lack of it - has brought you to where you are today

Indeed, the Power of our Mind, and Strength of our Will can lead us to discover many other things, that we sometimes refuse to believe in without definitive proof.

So maybe it's time to ask ourselves what proof do we actually need? And what in earthly terms is ever enough?

BEFORE

"The most beautiful thing we can experience is the mysterious. It is the source of all true art and all science. He to whom this emotion is a stranger, who can no longer pause to wonder and stand rapt in awe, is as good as dead: his eyes are closed."
Albert Einstein

I imagine it all really began when I was about 3 or 4 years old, although of course I didn't realise it then – or indeed for many years later.

My name is Jenni Shell - born in 1941, in the middle of the 2nd World War – the one that was never supposed to happen after the Great One of 1914/18. My mother told me I arrived in the middle of a thunderstorm, right in the midst of an "air-raid" so I suppose that was a befitting herald of things to come. Anyway, I guess I came to accept the more unusual aspects of life very early.

One of my first memories is seeing people running about shouting with saucepans on their heads, which seemed very funny at the time. Sometimes, my older brother put tin hats on our heads too, and we kept bashing them with a metal spoon because we thought it was all a game.

Then there were things they called "Doodle Bugs" that croaked angrily before floating silently like giant birds overhead, making everyone leap around and throw themselves onto the ground. They looked really silly when it rained, for they often got up covered in mud, but even the grown-ups seemed amused when that occurred – likely due to the relief of finding themselves still alive - although we children thought it was just part of the comical things that happened at times.

Oddly, many adults believe children don't remember much at such a young age. Bad memories can be crippling, and seeing some of the terrible things of war might have caused great harm. But we were lucky, for we had a wonderful grandmother who made fantastic imaginary stories out of all the terrifying and confusing ordeals.

I didn't like the Gas Masks, and screamed at first when told to wear one. It was the way everyone else looked in them that was so alarming, but Gran assured me that we were just rehearsing for a big circus, and everyone had to dress up as monkeys, so I didn't mind after that.

It was through my grandmother that I also learned not to be fearful of death. It was impossible to avoid the bombing, injury and sudden disaster during that time, and difficult to explain to a child why Jane's daddy had suddenly gone away without saying good-bye, or why Peter's mummy left him waiting alone in hospital while they took off his legs - not knowing she had died during the same bombing.

However, Gran explained that we all really lived in 2 places – one in the Sky with the Angels, called Heaven, and one in *"Their Garden"* called Earth. We couldn't all live in the Sky, or on Earth, at the same time, because there were far too many of us, so we had to share, and there was a big *"Change Over going on at the moment."*

The Sky was for *"looking down and resting"* – we were *"terribly big"* when up there - and the Earth was for *"doing things"*, and learning about the Garden and how to look after it. Then, when we were allowed back into the Sky/Heaven, we could tell God and the Angels all about it.

But she didn't explain why the 2 "nice ladies" - who sold "under counter" eggs at the top of the road - had to

3

be blown up rather than just fly away.   I knew that because I heard Grandpa telling Dad that they were still in the shop when it was 'smashed to blazes'.

Later that day my grandmother tried unsuccessfully to shield me from seeing a child's foot - still in its shoe - lying in the road amongst shards of glass.   When I asked about it she didn't answer me, but my brother decided that The Angels were probably trying out a rocket that went wrong, and the child had gone up to the Sky - so it didn't matter about the foot because it wasn't needed anymore.

It all seemed to make sense at the time, so in that simple way I guess I was shielded from the full horror of those events until I was much older.

It was only through my grandmother's magical and positive introduction to life, I was able to sustain my optimism amidst the many confrontational situations that later followed.

So, this is the story of an abandoned and isolated child, over-run by tragic family circumstances, and that of her own child – myself - so deeply moved by ensuing events that I sought to enter and try to understand the most complex and obscure of subjects.

Driven by heartbreak, confusion, and the everlasting question "WHY?" the road patiently led me from the reality of this earthly world into the far more difficult task of trying to comprehend the many other hidden and captivating realms of existence.

Nevertheless, this is just a story - the truth of which can be accepted or dismissed, according to how you perceive it - for it is indeed a personal story, written from my own perception of each event.

In order to protect their privacy, some of the names of the people have been changed.

1 GERTRUDE'S WORLD

My grandmother buzzed down the main high street, her chin aloft, with a look of contrived innocence on her face. I trailed behind, trying to keep up, for she seemed totally unaware of my presence. Being very young, the reactions of passers-by were deeply upsetting, for they kept staring and talking in amused whispers behind their hands. Trying to pretend I hadn't seen them, I scowled up at my grandmother, clutching hold of the sleeve of her voluminous blouse.

I adored my Gran; to me she was the best person in the world, and it didn't seem strange that she was wearing funny coloured socks under her long swirling skirt, and wasn't looking a bit like everyone else.

But her hat was horrid! It was a huge purple version of a floppy brimmed 'thing', attached precariously to a matching feather. She had seen it in a shop window, and immediately bought it. After plonking it unceremoniously on her head, she expected me to skip down the road beside her as if nothing had happened.

Hastily, I looked around to make sure none of my friends were about. Joyce Apples and Tricia Purdy would make me pay harshly if they saw us. They even put Jane Bottom in Coventry once because of her name, and wouldn't talk to me sometimes because their parents had told them that my mother was 'strange'.

Hanging back, I tried to keep as far away from Gran as possible but - as if suddenly aware of her parental duties - she grabbed my hand; clasping it to her ample bosom as we sallied forth across the road. It was then I decided enough was enough, and pulled hard on her arm, digging my heels into the pavement to make her stop. She threw a glance of minor frustration in my direction,

"Now, you're not going to be difficult are you dear?" she asked, looking remarkably like a taller and wider version of Margaret Rutherford from beneath the brim of her hat. The feather flapped around in the wind looking as if it was about to fly off.

"I don't like your hat – it's silly"

"Yes dear," she replied, absentmindedly pulling out an over large handkerchief from her bag. I yanked her again to make her look at me.

"But Gran, you're not listening, *it's your hat!* - It's...it's a wobbly shape, and it makes you look funny, and everyone is staring."

I waited for the repercussions, nervously tracing a crack in the pavement with my toe. Then to my amazement she gave me a big kiss on my cheek and burst out laughing.

"*Yes* dear, I know!" she chortled delightedly. "Isn't it marvellous! I've waited all my life to wear a hat like this and now I'm old I can do exactly as I please. I really don't care what people think!   Oh, isn't it just marvellous?"

I didn't think it was marvellous at all, and stood watching her sullenly, as she closed her bag with a loud snap.   I badly wanted to cry because I didn't understand what she meant, but she hugged me again, more gently this time, with a touch of sympathy in her smiling eyes.

"Don't worry dear, you couldn't possibly know what I'm talking about now, but you will one day, and when you get older you will remember this moment, and tell other people about it and....." she paused, "You know dear, it will make everyone laugh, and I'll be up there in heaven laughing at *them*, laughing at *you*, laughing at *me!*"

I remained silent, still very confused, and she nodded knowingly, "Just wait and see. Now come on, let's go home."

She stood upright, and trundled off at a pace of knots.

"You've got to understand dear" she said benevolently, "It's all 'Make Believe' you know. Nothing is really how it looks. My name is Gertrude, and this is *my* world!   I might look like an old battle-axe with an astonishing hat, but here inside there is a loving and happy heart.

"Come on, we'll soon be home. If you really can't bear to be with me, just hold my hand, and you can shut your eyes and make believe I'm not here."

Obediently I did as she suggested, and walked straight into a lamppost.

It was this simple innocence that was so wonderful but strange about my grandmother - she actually believed in 'Make Believe'. She said it made the world go round, and if you "thought" something hard enough it would happen in the end. I kept trying out the idea but it always seemed to go wrong for me.

I remember we took a two-hour journey to Brighton by bus once, to buy some doughnuts, and eat tomato sandwiches in an obscure little teashop off the main high street - why I don't know. I suppose because the journey was long and boring, Gran said that we should pretend we were on an underwater tour, and that the people weren't really people, but fishes in disguise. We found that great fun, until I got too close to an irritable octopus, who elbowed me in the mouth.

No, as much as I tried, I wasn't an easy convert to the imagination lark, and yet it seemed to work for everyone else.

I had a friend called Poppy Winters who was elevated to "Chief Protector" of the Fairies in "Dingle Dell" at the bottom of her garden, and danced around with them for hours. Yet, when I got fed up with looking - but not seeing anything - and decided to imagine I was a frog, I nearly drowned just because I hopped onto a lily pad in the pond.

Nothing seemed right somehow. If Gran believed in 'Make Believe', it had to be good, but what my brother insisted on calling 'Reality' seemed to be constantly getting in my way.

I had lots of dreams as a child, but even those didn't make me feel secure. One was of a striped snake that kept smiling at me from the bottom of my bed. I stroked it once and it felt real enough to frighten the life out of me. The other was about long white-gloved fingers that kept poking out through the sheets, and saying in a nasty voice, *"You've got a job to do."* It made me feel horrid, because I didn't like the sound of *"jobs"* very much.

Anyway, my grandmother was someone who loved to laugh, and imagine anything she wanted to make life exciting. She was a tremendous influence on my early life - although she was not my only relative of course.

I hardly saw anyone from my mother's side of the family as they lived some distance away and never came to visit, but my father's parents were right on our doorstep.

My grandfather was a beautifully dressed, quiet solemn old gentleman who stayed very much in the background, playing endless games of cricket with my elder brother. Gran was always pretending to make him give her "shillings" to take us to the pictures when we got fractious.

Grandpa had a sister called Aunt Dorothy who lived

in a pre-war house, with a labyrinth of rooms leading off each other - all infiltrated by the haunting smell of carbolic. She had four children who were my father's cousins. Three girls and a boy - who became a vicar - and they all talked at once. They were, in fact, a very religious family and one of them, Sheila, was my godmother.

In those days it was very important that the Godparents played an active part in the spiritual education of their charges. The girls of this family had many Godchildren and took their commitment very seriously. When they appeared on Sundays, neatly turned out in their best brown Burberry hats and 'sensible' shoes - waving bright, hand knitted woollen mittens, and chatting sociably to nobody in particular - it seemed like there were three hundred of them filling up all the available space.

Sunday was known as 'The Day of Church', although neither Gran, nor my parents ever went. Gran always classified herself as a 'distant believer', so it was left to Grandpa and the aunts to attend to our spiritual requirements. From a very young age my elder brother Dale and myself used to be escorted to the 10 o'clock service every week without fail, and filled with peppermints during the sermon to "keep them quiet".

Poor old God kept ringing the bell, but nobody appeared to notice or bothered to let Him in - or so it seemed to a child - for I was always looking but never saw Him, and when I asked why, they all went "Shhh"

So in the end, I decided to follow Gran's advice, and 'Make Believe'. Sometimes I imagined Him terribly large, but other times so tiny that I had to be ever so careful not to tread on Him.

I even tried to give Him a special name, but my godmother told me it wasn't allowed because it was not very 'respectful' to give Him ordinary names like Prince Philip – or Timothy after our cat. She said that God was the name everyone used, and that was good enough.

However, this didn't make sense to me, because I wanted a special God, so I secretly named Him a more reverend 'Mr Sauce', as Grandpa had called Him *'The Source of All Things'*, when I asked once.   Anyway, He became such a great friend in my imagination that He even joined in with the juice and biscuits at my Aunt's house, which were ladled out to all the godchildren around a huge table after the service.

All went well until one day I imagined God was a speck on my sandwich, and a horrid boy suddenly grabbed it from my plate and *ate* it - God and all!   It was a terrible experience, made worse by the laughter when I yelled out that Jacob Johnson had just eaten 'Mr Sauce'.

After much chortling, they tried to explain of course, but I didn't understand, for God was dead to me. I used to see Him in my head, even if they couldn't, and anyway I didn't like their kind of God, and wanted my own one back.

I went through a whole week of devastation until they came for me the following Sunday, and off we went as usual to church. I knew then that He must have survived or they wouldn't have bothered to take me. I was highly gratified for I always knew that *my* God was the best. I couldn't imagine where He was that day, but I knew He must be there waiting somewhere. Gran said that He'd probably made himself invisible to me as well, just in case I put Him on a sandwich again.

"You can't expect other people to see everything you can see," she said, as she washed my face in the scullery, and gave me a 'Carters little liver pill' – she always did that when she got over excited - "People see only what they want to see," she sighed.

"But why didn't He jump out of the way to stop Himself from being swallowed?" I queried plaintively.

"He *did!* He did dear," she patted me encouragingly. "It was just that you were so busy thinking He was eaten, that you didn't notice what He was really doing."

"I see," I mused, not seeing at all.

I still wasn't really certain that everything was okay until Gran shook me gently awake in the middle of the night with a cup of tea, which we sipped from a saucer, and told me to listen to the thunderstorm outside.

"Hear that noise?" she confided, as a heavy boom resounded across the countryside. "That was God dropping a chair. He's gone back home now and must be expecting guests, for He keeps moving the furniture around and lighting all the fires."

We sat for a long time peering through the curtains at the sheets of lightning flashing across the sky, and listening to the continuous rumble of beds and tables moving across the floor of Heaven. Finally, I fell asleep in her arms, and slept the sleep of my own world and my own reality.

And so I spent much of my younger years with someone who believed in "Make Believe", and somehow she managed to make me believe in it too, but I wasn't an easy child to inspire, for I was always asking "why?" to everything, which didn't help the fantasies much.

Coupled with that there were great chunks of me that felt so lonely inside. It was quite lonely at home though, for my mother always seemed to be very irritable, and rarely wanted to spend any time with us.

So I suppose to try to fill up the gaps, my brother and I were forever fighting.

Dale was 2 years older than me, but acted like the wisest owl in the book. Even at a very young age he informed me he was extremely old, and of course I believed him. He had a very innocent look about him, which concealed a wicked sense of humour, and, being the younger sibling, I became the obvious target of his interest; teasing me unmercifully whenever he saw the chance.

For myself, I thought he had an over big head that didn't seem to go with his body, but when I tried to tease him about it, he just informed me that he had a very large brain because he knew "everything", so his head *had* to be big otherwise his brain wouldn't fit.

Dale was a name I pretended to loath, but he insisted on calling himself Ed, which was worse. Coupled with that, he was always saying he was mending things, when in fact he was creating bombs and nasty inventions designed to frighten the living daylights out of me in particular. He and his horrible friend Sidney used to spend hours in the garage - eventually emerging like two inseparable Frankensteins, grinning from blackened faces before some devastating explosion or smell would blast us out of existence.

I never remember playing with my brother much, for it was more like a counter attack. Yet in a dreadful sort of way we used to protect each other with ferocious loyalty against any who dared interfere.

There was a boy called Lance, who lived across the road, and tried once to put my brother's head in a vice in my father's garage. In fairness he only did it after Dale had given me a crab apple, and sworn afterwards that it was laced with arsenic and I only had an hour to live. But I didn't care about that, and was just about to annihilate Lance with a mallet, when my mother intervened.

My poor, Mother. Many times in the years since my childhood, I've wondered that if we had made things easier perhaps life would have been different for her. My younger brother, Keith, was born at the end of the war. He was a gentle child; quiet, with a very loving disposition, but Dale and I must have been murder to deal with. We were both born during the war, which probably made things worse.

My mother's name was Honorah - a pretty name, although most people called her Nora. She was born in India, the daughter of an Italian mother, who died very young, and a Scottish father – an extremely clever man with an inventive mind

In her time, Mum was a lovely woman; a person who belied her age; slim, very youthful, with auburn hair, and sad grey eyes. She smoked a lot, as did my father – something totally acceptable in those days. She was deeply sensitive, and highly creative in the home, but never looked happy, and rarely laughed. I worried about her, for she frightened me when she was cross, and that seemed most of the time.

There wasn't much of a fantasy world for her I suppose, just the dreadful reality of trying to cope with two children under five and another pregnancy, during a terrible war, with little food and far less comfort in those stark years.

Later, I discovered how unhappy she was that her Italian maternal family were on the opposing side of the conflict, which must have compounded the issue.

My father was often away during Fire Service duties, and Mum seemed so frightened when he wasn't around. However, Dale and I weren't frightened at all, and my little brother Keith wasn't born until 1945, so he didn't care either.

In the midst of all this turmoil, I learned all about "The Baby Jesus" one night in the hastily erected air raid shelter clamped against the wall in the dining room. Dale, in one of his better moods, told me all about Him.   It was such a wonderful story for a child, except for ages afterwards I really believed that the Three Wise Men were scientists on camels, and the Star of Bethlehem was a bomb that went off before it could land.

Aeroplanes and sirens raged around us throughout that night, but I was oblivious to everything until the "all-clear" sounded, and my father came home.

It was only then I realised my mother had been crying silently beside me in the darkness and I'd never even noticed. I tried to kiss her, but she pushed me away, hiding her face, and I got fed up and went off in a sulk.

2 JOEY'S ASSIGNMENT

It was after the war that things seemed to get more difficult. I had spent much of my early years with my grandmother who also took Dale and I away for a time when we were evacuated. I don't remember much about it, except playing with rubber Lego bricks with a big boy called Robert who didn't seem to like us much. Then another time Dale locked us both in a "forbidden" room full of exciting looking toys in drawers. Even when Gran tried to coax Dale into putting the key under the door, he decided it was much more fun to stay in there, so we didn't come out for ages.

Coming home again was strange and unreal. Gran didn't see us for a while, to "allow you to settle in back home," as she said, but I don't think she and my mother saw eye to eye as she always spoiled us. Also, my grandmother didn't appear to really approve of my mother's ability to look after the family properly, because she kept leaving stews and pies on the doorstep - which my mother trod in once – and that didn't go down well at all.

So often the atmosphere wasn't good in the house and, as time went on, I started fretting about all sorts of silly things and often felt sick with worry over nothing at all. People upset me, or at least my friends did for they still put me into Coventry, and – just because I had curly hair – they started to call me "Curly cabbage" and said that my breath smelt of it too.

At 7 years old I was put to bed, supposedly with T.B. on my lung when I didn't even feel ill and, after 3 months of total rest, which was a nightmare, not only for myself but also my mother, I was allowed back to school.

Just over a year after that, my leg collapsed, in the middle of trying to slay Dale for putting a dead worm in my pencil box, and there I was back in bed again. I overheard my mother talking on the phone saying it was "Infantile Paralysis" and that they'd closed down the school. I was desperately upset. Surely my friends would never speak to me again. They'd probably put me in Coventry forever now.

I remember I got cross with God at that time for, if He knew, He should put a stop to it, but Gran said that He must have had good reasons for not doing so and, if I *really* believed I would get well soon, I would. She told me that something magical would appear that would make things a lot better in two days time.

So I waited, and tried to imagine being fit and strong with breath that smelt of roses, but even when a large teddy bear was delivered with a flourish to the door, exactly two days later, in the arms of my grandfather, I didn't feel better at all. In fact, I somehow felt worse, for I was old enough now to realise that it wasn't magic if Gran was making things happen. That didn't make sense. If she had to do that, it meant that even *she* believed that my illness had become a reality. And if she didn't believe in me being well, then how could I possibly imagine myself better?

On the third day, my father moved my bed out into the sunshine of the garden, for it was a hot summer that year, and I carried on waiting with grim determination. Gran had never been wrong yet. She may have got her dates muddled up that's all. I wouldn't eat my dinner, and didn't even care that my mother looked terribly white and tired, or that Dale was trying to make me laugh by pretending to hang himself in the summerhouse.

It was nearly four o'clock when I saw the bird perched on a telephone wire high up on the other side of the garden fence. Something squawked so loudly, it made me look up with a start, and there it was bouncing up and down, from one leg to another, as if doing a tightrope display for my own personal benefit. There was something glittering in its' beak and, as it waved in the sunlight I guessed it must be a Jackdaw because they were local round our way, and I knew they liked bright shinny things. I laughed, in spite of my miseries, and called to it. To my amazement, it came swooping down and landed straight on my shoulder, before dropping a small silver three-penny piece in my lap.

I picked it up turning it in the palm of my hand. The sunlight caught it through the rustle of the trees in the garden, and before I knew it, the bird hopped lightly onto the side of the bed, eyeing me with a piercing look before flapping off to return to the relative safety of his perch in the sky. And there he sat, looking and squawking until a chill came in the air, and my father came home from work to take me inside.

We called the bird Joey, and he returned every day for the whole of that summer. He became very tame and I was able to feed him eventually with crumbs from my hand. Gran said that she had been expecting him all the time, but I didn't really believe her. However, in my youthful innocence I became deeply convinced that this air-born magic had been sent especially for me. There was a look in his eye that seemed to hold more wisdom than a normal bird - something I thought I recognised - and it gave me courage; made me believe in myself, and find the will and determination to get well.

That autumn we discovered that Joey had a mate. She appeared one day dancing on the wire beside him and stayed a discreet distance while he swooped down to say his goodbyes. I knew he was going but didn't mind, for I was out of bed by then, and able to walk, so he'd done what he came to do.

I just hoped he understood when I thanked him. Gran said he did, and I had no reason to disbelieve her this time. I missed him dreadfully at first, and looked for him every summer after that, but of course he never came.

This experience was just one of a number of birds and cats that appeared in unusual circumstances as I continued on through life. In reality they were of course just birds and cats, but - from my perception over the years - they took on a much greater significance.

****

It wasn't too long afterwards that I started a new school, some distance away from us, and I travelled there by bike every day. It was one of those known as "High Schools", and we all wore uniform, including a wide brimmed straw hat in summer, which looked pretty awful.

What amazed me most was that I suddenly found myself very popular. Gone were the days of cabbage smelling breath and being in Coventry, which I had taken to be quite normal before. Now, everyone wanted to know me. Although I was still terribly thin, I had finally become fit and strong again, and seemed to have an uncanny brilliance at sport, which always makes people popular in schools. I loved the years that I spent there. They were full of laughter and exhausted teachers, trying to keep order. I remember thinking that it must be the worst job in the world to be a teacher.

During the time that I had been so ill, Mum seemed to get more and more nervous, uptight and withdrawn. I think Dad thought that when I was able to go back to school things would get easier for her, but over the same year, when I at last found my feet, she lost hers. She became obsessed with things that appeared unimportant, and used to cross-question everything in a confused and angry way. What exactly had people said to me this morning? Why was Dale looking like that? Why did I smile when I spoke just then? I felt an underlying feeling of terrible anxiety settling inside. Many were questions I couldn't really answer and, if I tried, she didn't seem to hear me anyway.

Often she would stand gazing into the eyes of some unseen being whilst having a secret conversation with them under her breath. Other times, she would go into a chaotic flurry of cleaning; clearing rooms time and time again, and polishing the springs on the beds, as if in a desperate attempt to get rid of something terrible that was there. Always she was unhappy. Raging in temper over nothing, and threatening us for what seemed no reason at all.

She had always smacked my brother and I since we were very young, and we both accepted it as nothing unusual - as children do I suppose. Dale, with his high intelligence and impish sense of humour seemed to antagonise her most of the time, so he definitely got the worst of it, yet he really was a perfectly normal child, and perhaps he only played around as a way of finding some lightness in a difficult little life. When she got really cross she used to shut him in the cupboard under the stairs, and I found her very frightening during those times.

When I look back, I realise that things got worse after my younger brother Keith was born. When he was tiny I used to try to protect him from her moods, but knowing now what I believe to be the root of her illness, I realise that this was not exactly necessary.

So our early childhood was indeed strange and unreal, for our experiences subjected us to two extremely different ways of looking at the world. However, although very contradictory in nature, it did give us a much more rounded approach to life.

Gran was full of fun, laughter and make believe. She loved nothing more than involving us in the wonder of things; whilst Mum's moods were very erratic; unpredictable and furious - then suddenly swinging the other way as if in a frantic desire to redress the balance. I found her really hard to understand for I loved her very much, and she was so gentle and sweet in her better times, but my deep sensitivity to events caused great sadness and questioning pain.

Life became very difficult at home, and Dale and I spent more and more time out of the house. I found great comfort in my school friends, and Dale by that time had decided he was going to be a "scientific inventor" and started experimenting in other people's houses.

My kid brother Keith was only five, and lived with Gran most of the time, whilst Dad never talked about these things - probably because he worked very hard and there was little he actually knew about what was going on, anyway.

3 MY SACRED VOW

I was 10 years old when everything seemed to suddenly turn upside down, and the series of events that followed have left a scar on all of us that will probably last forever. It was a Friday, and I got back from school early, having been sent home because I felt unwell.

My mother was in a terrible state in the kitchen. Her face and eyes were puffy and swollen, and the oven door was open, with a cushion placed inside. Indeed, there was a dreadful atmosphere of distress and, although she had her back to me when I walked in, I knew immediately that something was about to happen that would radically change my life. I looked at the time. It was 3 o'clock, and it was somewhere around that moment that I grew up.

I can't say that I really knew exactly what was happening. I was terribly confused, but felt the need to urgently run to someone for help, and opted for next door. During the rest of the day the world fell into chaos.

My father came home and Mum was desperately upset and they argued. Finally she drew him out into the hall and pointed to some scribbling that Keith had drawn with his childlike hand on parts of the wall still suffering from war damage. Bewildered and curious, I joined them. Mum was desperate to prove something to Dad and, clinging onto his hand, she began to make complete sentences out of the gibberish of my brother's drawings. I looked on, and saw my father's smile of irritated patience change slowly to the blank shadow of disbelief, and then realisation.

He pushed me hastily into the back room, and as the door clicked quietly behind, I sat down heavily beside Dale who was sprawled across the table doing his homework.

"Go away." He said bluntly.

"I can't. They've shut me in here." I was still shocked and confused. "I'm sure that Dad thinks Mum's gone mad." Dale scowled at me over his glasses.

"Sometimes you're so boring," he observed. I threw a pencil at him, and glowered as hard as I could.

"It's true I tell you! You don't even care do you! All you're interested in are your soppy Bunsen burners and test tubes!"

"Of course I care you stupid girl," he retorted, firing an elastic band at a picture on the wall, before adding more quietly, "What is madness anyway?"

"How should I know?"

"It's all to do with people making things up that *aren't* there. That's madness." He announced patronisingly.

"Oh yes? So you're so clever! Where do "make believe" and imagination come in then?"

"Oh cripes.... here we go again," he groaned loudly. "For your information, madness is making things up that AREN'T there, but believing they ARE, and Make Believe is making things up that AREN'T there, but knowing they're NOT. See stupid."

I pondered for a while.

"That doesn't make sense."

"I know....".

"What then?" I asked finally.

22

He sighed impatiently.

"The answer, dear child, is to deal only in *facts*. Facts don't change, but "pretending" changes all the time. That's where people go wrong. Reality is *always* there, but Make Believe changes because we only *imagine* it in the first place.

See that fist?" he waved a black looking thing under my nose. "If I hit you with that, you'd certainly know it! *That's reality. Science is reality*. It proves things. Anyway", he trailed off, "Lots of people are mad …".

I thought again for a while. "But we are told that God is "real". We *feel* Him, but don't really *see* Him, do we? So how do we know that He's not just imagination or that *we* are actually mad? And who made up the rules about madness anyway?"

"Oh do shut up!" I ducked as he aimed another rubber band at me before going back to his work.

****

As the summer of my illness had been scorching hot, so the winter of the first year of my mother's illness was bitterly cold. My father tried to hang on for a while, to see if there would be any improvement, but she became worse and worse. Finally, two men in white coats came to the door with a doctor, and they signed papers in the hall. It was a terrible experience, for they dragged her away when she didn't want to go, and she begged them so pathetically not to take her.

My father seemed to just stand there helplessly doing nothing, and I couldn't understand why. He made me go upstairs to prevent me seeing the worst of it, but I watched from the window as the ambulance drew away, and cried for the crass stupidity and loneliness of adulthood, which I was too young to comprehend or do anything about.

Dale had gone down with 'flu the day before, and he was being looked after by Gran. Keith had been staying too, because things were so difficult at home. So I was there on my own, and still feeling terribly upset and confused. My father came upstairs to speak to me after Mum had been taken, but I didn't want to talk to him really. I just sat dumbly on the bed.

"Your mother's very ill," he said gently.

"I know," I swung my leg, repeatedly kicking the foot of the bed.

He tried again.

"Do you understand what's wrong?"

"Not really. She's mad isn't she?"

"Well, not quite dear. She's just having a nervous breakdown, that's all. She hasn't had an easy life."

"Dale says lots of people are mad."

My father smiled wanly.

"Yes, I think he's probably right."

"Well, how do we know which is which?"

"We don't really, I suppose, but doctors know these things." I could feel myself getting really cross.

"Who are these doctors? They might be mad people pretending they are not."

My father suddenly looked desperately tired and irritated. "Come on dear," he said firmly. "Let's go and see your grandparents."

My grandparents took the news with extreme shock, and it was only then that I realised that Dad had kept my mother's condition secret from them for all this time. I remember we stood on the landing on the way up to Dale's room, and Grandpa grabbed hold of the stair-rail to stop himself from falling.

I was astounded at their reaction, for Gran of all people should have understood. I wanted desperately for her to explain it all to me, but everything got impossible all at once. Dale rushed out to the bathroom to be sick, and Keith appeared from another room on hands and knees pretending to be a bus conductor and pushing a large dinky toy in front of him, going,

"Beep! Beep! Ding! Ding! Okay, Bert!"

Gran bustled around making cups of tea and flapping all over the place, and there, amongst the hubbub my grandfather remained forgotten, making no fuss, but sitting quietly on the stairs. That was the last time I saw him alive, for he had a massive heart attack and died in hospital just over a week later. Everything had obviously been too much.

After that, things became a little hazy for a bit. Gran took Grandpa's death so badly that my father was forced to send Keith to stay with the aunts, and keep Dale and I back home, so she could be alone with her thoughts, and her pain.

****

I don't know what day it was that Dad took us to see Mum in hospital, but it was before Grandpa's funeral. I think it was something he always regretted, but who knows, if it hadn't happened, I doubt if I would be writing this now.

I had never seen the inside of a hospital to remember, except when my kid brother was born, but I was soon to discover that a mental institution looked like a normal hospital only it was far worse.

Of course, things are very different today, but at that time, the walls were bleak and grey, and the floors were damp and cold for the heating was far from adequate. I could hear muffled screams coming from the padded cells that lined the corridors. One door was tied up with a piece of bandage and looked dangerously near breaking point. I felt glad that Keith hadn't been allowed to come, and kept very close to Dale and my father, for I was frightened and horrified that my mother should be kept in there.

A nurse led us into an enclosed room, which looked rather like a surgery, and a quietly spoken doctor with a friendly face approached us kindly, saying,

"She's just coming out of treatment. I don't know whether you can see her yet. I will go and find out"

He pushed the adjoining door. It was one of those that swings open and automatically closes behind - only this one didn't. I was standing at the front, and unfortunately it held its position long enough for me to get a glimpse of my mother as she was being hastily removed from what looked like a board with circular "things" attached to her head. It was just at that moment she saw us, and called out with the most agonising cry to my father that chilled me to the bone.

In those split seconds I saw it all - the terrible torment, futility and emptiness of finding herself alone in the midst of this terrifying ordeal. She was struggling to free herself, holding out her arms towards us, with a stark empty hopelessness in her eyes, tears streaming down her face. In stunned silence I stood and saw her hair was grey.

The next few minutes seemed to be cut completely from my world. My mind refused to take it in; to know what it meant; to react or do something about it. An ice cold pain gripped my stomach, and I found myself trembling, sobbing and shouting as Dale dragged me back up the corridors and out into the winter rain.

I shivered and stopped crying as suddenly as I'd started, and stared at him as he pulled up the collar of my coat. He was pure white and his hands were shaking as he tried to hold me tight and get some warmth between us.

"You went berserk in there," he said finally. "It's no use going berserk. You're always so hysterical. It's no good being hysterical. They'll put *you* away next."

I looked at him blankly.

"What have they done to her?"

"I don't know."

"You're lying! You do know, I heard you talking to Dad before we came out."

"It's nothing," he said uncertainly. I was suddenly furious.

"Nothing! What do you mean nothing? You saw her. Her hair's gone grey. Do you call that nothing?"

He studied me silently for a while, before saying slowly,

"They call it electrical treatment. They put those wires on her head and send an electrical current through to make her better."

I thought I'd misheard him for a minute. I was grappling with electrocution and other such horrors.

"And what does that do? How does it make her better?" He shrugged his shoulders.

"Don't ask me. Talk to Dad about it. I think it makes her have a fit and it stops her imagining things."

"Imagining what?"

"I don't know! How am I supposed to know?"

"But we all imagine things. Gran says it's what makes the world go round. How come Mum's not allowed to?"

"I told you, I don't know!" He still looked terribly white and glowered at me fiercely. "*Why don't you shut up?* You always ask stupid questions. All the time, all the time, questions."

"And *you*, jolly genius, *claim* to know all the answers!"

"I do - when it comes to facts. I told you, I deal in *facts*. "Make Believe" is stupid! Imagination is stupid! Everything's stupid, and particularly you!"

"Well I intend to find out!"

"Go ahead, crack-pot. They'll just call you mad too."

I turned my back on him then, refusing to listen, and shut myself away in my own private world in my mind. There had to be an answer somewhere, and I secretly whispered a solemn vow to the sky,

"There must be an answer, and by all that is Holy, I *will* find it!"

4 FACT OR FANTASY

I don't remember my father coming out of the hospital, or us travelling home, for I was thinking all the time. Thinking about what to do, and wishing I were older so I could do it, whatever 'it' was.

Everyone was terribly quiet, especially my brother, for without a doubt the sequence of events must have been both bewildering and heart breaking for him also. But Dale didn't allow himself to show these things. He was the family's oldest child - his father's son - and thanks to God for that, because he was indeed a wealth of support for my poor dear father throughout the following years.

I carried on thinking well into the evening. Everything was in a turmoil, going round and round in my head, until I couldn't stand it anymore and went downstairs to find my father, who was sat silently alone in the front room. He looked as if he had been crying and he hadn't even bothered to light the fire.

I knelt down beside him and gave him a tentative hug, trying to forget that I found it hard to forgive him for letting Mum suffer so much.

"What's wrong with Mum?" I asked.

"She's ill."

"I know, but what with?"

"She imagines things."

"I know, but what?" He turned towards me and heaved a heavy sigh. At last he spoke.

"She has what we call "Delusions". That means she believes things that don't happen."

"But how do we know they don't happen? She might be able to see things other people can't. Gran says children can do that sometimes". He sighed again.

"I'm afraid it's not as easy as that dear," he said gently. "The things that she sees or believes worry and upset her, and because they're not true, we can't do anything for her except to give her drugs or electrical treatment to try to jolt her back to reality."

So here I was again, back to the same old question.

"What is reality, Dad? I just don't understand. Do we always know it when we see it, or perhaps it could be somebody else's 'Make Believe?'"

For some reason he smiled before replying.

"I think it could be sometimes, but you know it really doesn't matter in the long run. Imagination is one thing - it's wonderful for writers and artists. Even people like ourselves can live in a fantasy world if we want to, but, if it starts to bother us to the extent that it affects our normal lives and those of others around us, then society has to step in and try to do something about it."

"You mean make us conform?"

"If you like to call it that."

I didn't like to call it that. My mother had so often said she saw things that we didn't, and having grown up with the idea of "Make believe", I couldn't understand why that mattered if it was real to her.

"Dad, how would you feel if you had a red coat, and everyone said it was black? Would you believe them or yourself?"

"Well, it wouldn't worry me dear," he said after a moment's silence. "I would probably prefer to have a black coat anyway. The point is that it wouldn't worry me what people said, but it worries your mother."

I felt really confused, and wished I hadn't started the conversation. There always seemed to be questions that never had simple answers.

I said goodnight and went even more fretfully to bed, lying tossing and turning for what seemed like hours, trying to put my own thoughts alongside my mother's and failed. How could we say if she had delusions, or was just seeing things differently?

I put my hand out and placed it hard against the wall. It felt cold and damp with condensation from the heat of my electric fire. The bed I was lying on was soft beneath my weight. Both these things were real enough. They wouldn't move if we tried to walk through them, so they must be real. I thought that my belief in God was real enough also, yet I couldn't touch Him like a wall - or was it only me who couldn't?

Ghosts walked through walls, or did people who saw them imagine them? If a ghost frightened me, and everyone told me I was making it up, and then shut me in a room with it, I figured it would make me pretty upset.

So how could we possibly know whose belief was correct? There had to be an answer somewhere. Forcing people to change their thinking couldn't be right, surely? I started to cry quietly with anger, resentment and futility. Was everything I had believed in real, or was it all nonsense? Was my grandmother wrong in her ideas, or was Dale wrong?

I began to sob hopelessly, trying to ease the pain in my stomach that threatened to tear me apart. Then, suddenly through my tears I heard the door open behind me, and a hand, warm and comforting, gripped me firmly on the shoulder. I felt the relief of peace spread through me, and turned to put my arms round my father - but he wasn't there. Nobody was there!

I sat up in bed in shock. The steady glow of the fire reflected shadows throughout the room – but nobody was there. The door was still closed and I could hear the gentle creaking of the house as it settled in for the night. Somebody had definitely put a hand on my shoulder, but they weren't there – or were they?

Slowly I found myself smiling. Nobody could convince me that nobody had put a hand on my shoulder, yet it seemed that nobody had - Or nobody would believe that they had! How crazy this was! I turned over ready for sleep for the first time in many days.

Anyway, whatever it was, it had made me feel so much better - but I didn't think I would tell anyone about it - except Gran, perhaps.

****

The following day I went to see Gran. She was sitting, looking out of the upstairs window, and watched me without moving as I came up the tiled garden path, and through the two low privet hedges situated either side of the open front door. She still didn't get up when I walked into the room, but carried on sitting, as if studying the passers-by while they bustled about their business up and down the busy main road. I put my arms round her from behind, and gave her a soft kiss on the cheek, feeling like an intruder into her private world.

Drawing up a chair, I sat down silently beside her.

"Harnam is very lonely without your grandfather," she said quietly.

"Harnam" was the name she had given the house -

a large rambling place, covered in ivy, with wide windows and set back from the road. It was full of big comfortable chairs, and intricate pieces of furniture, including a huge mirror suspended across the dark sideboard in the dining room, and an impressive brass disc hung in the hall – a residue of family travels. She had a wonderful collection of oddities, but her most prized possession was a picture of my father aged two years old, sitting on a pile of books. It was proudly placed by the front door, and was so beautifully drawn it was easily mistaken for a photograph.

Gran would never allow the ivy to be trimmed, except round the windows, because she liked to watch the birds making their nests in it during the springtime. She used to make issues about the giant spiders that lived there, and sometimes came in to "eat crumbs from the larder" but I think she rather liked them secretly. I was frightened of them when I was small, but Gran just laughed at me and told me to put a glass over them and 'walk them to the door'.

"You're much bigger than them," she used to say. "Just imagine how frightened they must be of you."

I hesitated for a while, looking at my grandmother's sad resigned face, and tried to think of the right thing to say. I couldn't, so I didn't say anything, and carried on looking out onto the street.

A woman whom Gran had christened, "Mrs Ump Thump" - because she spoke so strangely - trundled past and waved glibly, her red woolly hat and scarf threatening to take off and smother her in the wind. Her descriptive name was most un-politically correct by today's standards, but in those days nobody minded a bit – least of all the lady herself. I guess these things paled into insignificance compared to the more important issues of hardship that came from the war and beyond. As this jolly little lady sailed past, Gran and I would have normally laughed, but it didn't seem funny that day.

Finally, my grandmother spoke as if to nobody. "I'm sending Grandpa to church on Sunday before the funeral. He wanted to go last week, but I wouldn't let him. I made him take some sausages up for you children instead. I wish I'd let him go - he wanted to go - but I didn't know..." Her voice disappeared into nothing.

I stumbled to think of something to say that would help.

"You've always believed in God, Gran. Perhaps he's with God now?" She took a deep breath and pulled herself together before patting my hand.

"Yes, I expect he is dear. Someone was trying to tell me something last night. I was sitting here in the darkness, looking out at the stars and wondering about your mother and everything, and crying, and asking silly questions. Then all of a sudden someone came in and put a hand on my shoulder and I felt much better. I thought it was your father at first, but there was nobody there - I think it was probably God."

I was amazed and delighted, and couldn't restrain from telling her.

"That happened to me too last night, Gran! I thought it was Dad too, but there was nobody there! That happened to me too!" My voice rose in excitement.

"Did it, dear?" She didn't sound surprised. I thought for a while before saying,

"Gran? I've been wondering... was it imagination?" She looked round at me and smiled confidently,

"Oh no! It was so real, it must have been real!"

So was that it? Imagination isn't imagination once it becomes strong enough to really feel it - to know it exists? Then it becomes reality? So much for my brother's facts.

But that didn't answer the problem for my mother. Her imagination had become reality to her, yet everyone was telling her otherwise. No wonder she was so upset all the time. Restraining people was surely not the answer, but there had to be an answer.

My grandmother's voice broke into my thoughts.

"Don't ever get old, dear."

"But I thought you loved being old."

"That was when I really believed I was young in spite of my age; just 'thinking' that made me young. At the moment I feel very old, so I am old. It's all in the mind, dear. If ever we have a job to do in life, it's to believe in ourselves. Once we do that, we can start to believe in all the strange inexplicable things in this world - but if we lose faith in our own judgements we have lost everything. All the Gods in Heaven won't help us then. If your mother didn't mind what anybody thought of her ideas she wouldn't be in hospital now"

She paused for a moment…"You know, dear, a lot of people think I am very odd. I am a bit eccentric I suppose, but I really don't care what people think." She smiled mischievously and launched into a quote – *"All the world is queer, me dear, except thee and me… and even thee is a little queer!"*

I laughed as I remembered the astounded stares of people as Gran galloped along in her purple hat, all those years ago. Maybe it is the doubts and the worry, not what we imagine that causes the problems? But I didn't want to think about it anymore.

The funeral of my grandfather went off okay. He duly appeared in church the day before, while all my aunts and us youngsters gathered together as usual. My father came too for the first time that I can remember. He cried during the service, and I can only appreciate now how very alone he must have felt right then.

I watched everyone file up to take communion, and wondered if Grandpa was sharing it with them as Gran had hoped, or if he was far away cavorting amongst the stars enjoying his new life. It didn't occur to me to feel grief. Perhaps I had felt too much of late, but all I know is that I didn't cry and I didn't want to either.

I was still engrossed in where my mother was and how she was feeling. I knew Grandpa was all right, but what about her? She still had to live in this world, and I couldn't see her now, because Dad wouldn't let me go there after the first time.

5 THE SÉANCE

It was sometime in early January when Gran hustled me into the front room at "Harnam" before peering at me secretly and saying,

"I'm sending you to a 'Séance'. You don't mind going for me do you, dear?"

"What's a 'Séance'?" I asked.

"Oh, it's a place where you meet ghosts and things." She waved her arms in the air as if by description. "I must talk to your grandfather and find out how he is."

"Yes, but wouldn't it be better if you went? You'd know what to say to him." I felt very unsure.

"No, I don't think so. I don't feel very well at the moment, and I might cry. It's better if you go. Besides you like ghosts don't you? I thought you liked them."

"I've never met one!"

"Well, now's your chance. You don't have to talk to them. They talk to you. They won't hurt you, you know. After all, it's only Grandpa and he wouldn't hurt a fly."

"What does Dad say about it?" I asked, feeling my father would have a lot to say.

"He say's it's alright, but I'm not sure he was really listening. I told him it was like church"

"Oh!" I was perfectly sure my father hadn't been listening, and was greatly surprised, but in retrospect I guess he had too much else to worry about other than the hazards of my grandmother's excursions. He was used to her doing strange things.

"You will go for me, won't you, dear?" She cajoled gently, "I thought of asking Dale but he doesn't "believe", and you've got to believe or it won't work. Besides he might let a stink-bomb off in the middle and that wouldn't do at all."

"Well, yes I'll go." I was beginning to be quite interested, if just a little scared, but I trusted that Gran would never let any harm come to me.

"Good. I knew you would! So that's settled then. You're going tonight with Maisie, a friend of Mrs Ump Thump."

Seven o'clock arrived and so did Mrs Ump Thump's friend. She looked rather a peculiar woman to me, with a bright orange headscarf and Jesus sandals. We had to get a bus to the venue for an eight o'clock meeting, so we left straight away.

As we walked off into the night I heard Gran calling after me,

"Don't forget, dear. If he talks in a loud, boomy voice, it's still your grandfather."

****

We arrived at the hall with little time to spare. I hadn't seriously thought of what it would be like, but certainly didn't expect to see the inside of a real church - pews and all.

I sat down tentatively on the edge of my seat, waiting for things to begin, and looked round for Grandpa, wondering if he would suddenly sit down beside me.

There seemed to be lots of people there, all talking in loud voices, which I thought was very irreverent. Then a jolly-faced woman walked in, wearing a short black cloak dotted in sequins. She looked rather surprised in her two-toned hair - which rose high in a quaff under her hat.

We all stood up. She smiled benignly and said hello to a Mrs Lloyd who was sat smirking at the back, before announcing the first hymn. That was surprising too. Fancy singing hymns to ghosts! There was still no sign of Grandpa....

And so the service began, for it was indeed a service and very like those in church, except that everyone sang out of tune, and the pianist kept losing notes on the piano where the damp had crept in. She was very old, and fell asleep twice, but somebody had obviously been put beside her to prod her awake each time we sang. We seemed to be getting up and sitting down for hymns and prayers for ages, and I almost gave up hope of seeing Grandpa, when all at once everything stopped and we sat down again.

The woman with two-toned hair closed her eyes, and we waited. After a few minutes silence, when I was beginning to fidget, she suddenly opened her eyes and pointed straight in my direction.

"It's for you." She said. I turned round to look at the woman behind me, and she turned round to look at the person behind her, who did the same. Then we all looked back to the front again, wondering whom she was pointing at.

"It's for you" she repeated. "The young girl in the red cardigan. It's for you."

"Say God bless you," hissed Maisie in my ear.

"Why?"

"Just say it!" She hissed again. "There's a message coming through for you."

"God bless you," I said obediently, feeling a total idiot.

"Have you got a grandmother called Bobby?" The two-toned woman shut her eyes again. I was utterly amazed.

"No, her name's Gertrude, but they call her Bobby sometimes."

"Did she have a horse?"

"Pardon?"

"I said – *did she have a horse?*", she accented the words.

"No" I stuttered. "At least I don't think so." You never knew with Gran.

"Well, I've got a horse here, who says his name is Bob."

"Oh" I looked around fearfully, wondering what I was going to see. Everyone was staring at me and smiling, like adults do to children, so I looked back hastily to the front. Mrs Two-Tone continued.

"Yes, he says your grandmother used to look after him when she was young, and she'll remember him."

"Oh" I repeated.

"Yes, and I've got someone called Bill or William here, who says he's your grandfather."

That was right! She was right! How on earth did she do that? I beamed in excitement and forgot to answer her.

"Can you take that?" asked the woman.

"Where to?" I ventured uncertainly.

"I mean do you *understand* that?"

"Oh, yes thanks."

She continued. "Your grandfather says to tell Bobby not to worry. He's very happy and shortly she will hear some good news."

"Gosh, thank you." I was gratified, but wished Grandpa would appear.

"Yes, and he's also got a message for you. He says do you remember your dreams about fingers?"

"Yes?"

"Well, you've got to take notice of them."

"How?" I asked nervously, not liking the statement, but she'd gone back to sleep and ignored my question.

The woman with the two-toned hair carried on giving messages to other people for quite sometime, but as they were very personal to them, it didn't mean much to me.

At first I was bowled over by everything, but after a while I got a little suspicious. Maisie must have known about the recent events in our family, and she could have told the woman who gave messages? I would have felt a lot better if Grandpa had appeared and told me himself. I supposed that would have been the only kind of proof that Dale would accept.

It still didn't explain about the horse. I'd never even heard of a horse called Bob. I'd have to ask Gran. And anyway, what on earth would a horse want to give a message for? It wasn't even a very interesting one.

Back home, Gran sat me down with crumpets and

tea thick with sugar.

"Did you see Grandpa?" She asked, when she couldn't contain herself any longer.

"Well, not exactly, but I did get a message from him." So I told her what had happened. She seemed very pleased, but when I told her about the horse she became very excited.

"There you are, you see! Nobody knew about my horse, Bob, so they got him to send a message just to prove it works. He was a good horse my horse, Bob. That was how I got my nickname Bobby when I was young. Grandpa knew about him, and so did your father, but I never told *you*, did I?"

"No," I answered, still a little suspicious.

"There!" Gran said knowingly. She seemed more pleased about that than hearing about Grandpa. "It's nice to have some proof, even if we do believe."

"Gran, what's an Aura?" I asked, remembering a woman looking like a codfish in a pink hat, who had bounded up to me after the service, declaring,

"My child, your Aura!"

"I'm not too sure dear," she mused. "I think it's a light that glows out of the body or something."

"Well, I've got one, and it's big and green."

"Good Lord!" she said astounded. "Well, we learn something everyday."

For weeks afterwards I was terribly excited about everything, even if a little unsure of how exactly it had happened on the evening. I remember I kept telling people that I had been to a séance in church, which upset my aunts very much at the time. And of course, later I was to discover that I had been to a Spiritualist Church, and therefore it wasn't a séance at all.

****

It was six months before my mother returned from hospital. I suppose the good news we heard, as Grandpa had promised, was that her condition was controllable provided she stayed on drugs for the rest of her life. To me it wasn't good news at all, and almost impossible to accept, for suppression seemed to be a dreadful substitute for a cure.

As I grew older, and started to learn more, Dad and I talked for many long hours about it, but I think I often made him frustrated and angry by my continuous arguments. However, being true to his naturally sensitive nature, he did his best to accommodate me and appease my frustration in a simple, yet logical way. He explained that he understood what I was trying to say, and in many ways he agreed with me, but I suppose he appreciated more than I did the perilous dangers of allowing Mum's mind to run free and without control.

"It would be terribly cruel to allow her to suffer that torment," he once said.

"But isn't the torment of being drugged against her will, and knowing she's in a mental hospital worse? Surely, she needs help to find happiness in her own way, not suppression of her pain, just so we can all pretend it doesn't exist. Is that an answer?"

"Of course it isn't," he replied. "But who's going to give her this cure and how? The drugs take away the worries and the pain. Believe me, the doctors know best."

So I suppose that was it. My father believed in the wisdom of the medical profession, but I wasn't sure.

They were, after all, people like anyone else, and since I knew that one of my mother's so called 'delusions' revolved around doctors, I felt all the more uneasy. What if they had all closed ranks against her, to protect themselves from something? Maybe she knew something about doctors that we didn't. I put that point to Dad, but he assured me that, whatever the truth, it didn't matter, for it shouldn't have made her ill.

I couldn't understand that at all. To me, anybody, however normal, could be made ill by the frustration, anger and resentment of not being believed – especially if they were telling the truth.

But of course I later came to realise that my father was right in so many ways. Whatever it was, illusion or reality, it had made her ill, and it was an illness that went beyond the guidelines of reason that most would understand. She saw surreptitious signals made by strangers as they passed innocently in their cars; misunderstood the simplest of statements, and became inexplicably obsessed by the number 3, as well as certain colours and objects. That was only part of it. The sudden dramatic changes and violence of her suffering, unless she took her medication, were perhaps more intolerable to us than they were to her.

Gradually I started to give up the fight. It was easier to let her stay on the drugs, and eventually we got relatively used to the routine of her going in and out of hospital and living for much of the time in a vague and distant dream world.

Time went on, wounds began to heal, and Dale, Keith, and I travelled on to more grown up times.

6 GROWING UP

After Grandpa's funeral, my father took his place in church every Sunday. He became very involved and interested in religion generally, and studied all aspects of it. He told me that it gave him many profound realisations about life and the process of existence.

After a while, he became a Brother of St. Andrews and got deeply immersed in theosophical teachings. It seemed that he was trying to find his own answers to the problem of this "reality" that had hit our family so hard, and throughout the continued years of my mother's illness he grew greatly for me in stature and understanding.

Most people loved my father. His name was Geoffrey – called after an obscure family friend. Born an only child, I suspect Dad was a bit spoiled by Gran, for she absolutely adored him. She indicated he was quite wild and brash when younger - and something of a flirt – for in his youth he was extremely blonde, with sparkling blue eyes, and strong in stance, which women found greatly attractive. Dad was a drummer in his own band in the 1930s and just loved to be at the centre of things. People found him very easy to get on with, for he had a great sense of humour like his mother before him, but it could never be said that he was as "quirky" as her.

Gran said later that his experiences of bringing up a family in the war, and my mother's subsequent breakdown, had turned him into someone far more serious and responsible than she expected him to be, which seemed to greatly sadden her.

It must have been very daunting for him, but not once did he complain of the stress and difficulties of trying to cope and - although I was of little help through this time - there was no criticism of the pressure.

Through his appreciation of humour and his solid dependability he became the cornerstone of my later life, and I looked on him as more of a friend than a father who was well aware of his own inadequacies and tolerated me for mine.

Often he used to laugh at himself and his absentmindedness, and always he was gentle and considerate, putting others before himself. In those years he taught me more about tolerance than I've learned in a lifetime since, and through his example I became aware of the true meaning of patience and understanding of another's viewpoint.

"I don't complain because I never mind, dear," he said once. "There's nothing very remarkable or good about that. It's just an attitude of mind. I've nothing to complain about."

"Others would think you have." I argued.

"Others are entitled to their own opinions," he replied. "But our job is not to make judgements of others. We should only make judgements of ourselves, and how *we* feel within a situation. It doesn't really matter whether we are right or wrong. All that matters is what *we feel*. The answer is very simple. It's all in the mind. You must always remember to believe in yourself and not the voices of others."

"I suppose that's where Mum went wrong?" I asked, thinking how like Gran he sounded.

"In some ways perhaps, but there's more to it than that. She, like many people, can't see that everything matters, but nothing matters when it comes down to how much we allow it to invade our lives. It's the way we look at it that makes the difference."

****

Dad gave up the study of religion just as suddenly as he had started. He didn't talk about it much, except to say that he felt it was no longer necessary to go to church. Later, I was to fully appreciate that church is not the only place where we can show our serious intent, and maybe our own personal spiritual space is more acceptable for expression.

As for Dale, he, of course, took the pathway of science as expected. He remained determinedly of the same opinion as when young. The only reality for him lay in facts, and over the years it became obvious that our mother's illness had such a lasting affect that it determined the future of both our lives, as well as that of our father. It was just that we each chose different pathways.

My brother's study of science, took him in its own way, into the probing of the mind, just as did my father's study of religion, and for myself, I suppose I lurked somewhere in the middle - in the world of psychology and imagination. We used to spend many long, but confrontational discussions whilst Dale and I were still at home - particularly about our different opinions of "reality" - when it came to the comparison between science and religion or sanity and insanity.   Dale announced once, in the middle of an argument about the latter.

"Did you know that a chemical reaction in the brain could affect your whole process of thought?"

"So?" I replied.

"So, that means that some people can't be in control of their attitude of mind because they may have too much of a chemical which causes them to have delusions in the first place."

"In that case, why don't you scientists produce something that solves the problem?"

"Well, what do you think the drugs are for?" He enquired, looking rather smug.

****

Dale's experimenting days of the past had held him in good stead, and he went on to make a very successful career. It was a proud moment when he attained a 1st in Civil Engineering at Imperial College, London, and a Master of Science Degree in Transport. He continued to dislike "vagaries", and bluntly refused to believe anything that couldn't be proven. "Proof" to him was the only reality, so he didn't seem impressed by my growing interest in Astrology or the psychology of human emotion, and in our younger days, had the infuriating habit of always lowering his voice when in a heated discussion, whilst advising me not to get hysterical.

His body had caught up with his head by then, but to me he was still someone whose enormous brain probably knew the answer to the universe and certainly deserved a modicum of respect. Yet extraordinarily, to see him walking around in over large trousers, shrunken hand knitted sweaters, and comfortable slippers - looking remarkably like the true, storybook version of the absentminded professor, curly hair all over the place, and muttering unintelligible formulas - one could be excused for thinking that, far from being a "realist", he was perhaps a little confused.

In spite of our youthful banter, I have always thought of Dale with immense affection. As proven when younger, he had a great sense of humour and never minded being the source of amusement at times. My most vivid teenage memories of him are with a book clutched in one hand, and very weird looking contraptions in the other - whilst tripping everyone up with cascades of wires and evil looking instruments draped around the house - or flat on his back under the car, listening to "The Goons", who were his idols during those years. And sometimes I would see him sunk in a deckchair by the summerhouse, so engrossed in fierce concentration on his book that he was quite unaware it was raining.

It must have seemed to outsiders, that we were indeed a houseful of mental cases, for it can never be said that any of the family lacked a sense of humour. The ludicrous situations of drama in which we often found ourselves, is a book in itself, and I learned early that one of the greatest teachers in life is that of laughter. Religion and science, tragedy and comedy, found it very easy to walk alongside each other in our house, and all these experiences have been a foundation for my understanding today.

****

In the old days, I used to think that Keith was different. He was younger than us; had no memories of the war; seemed calmer and less outspoken than Dale and I and, as said before, our mother was far less irritated by him, than us.

Keith seemed to take life quite seriously, and didn't play around at fighting or teasing people like we did. Being very sensitive and gentle, it was assumed he was more of an observer of events at home than actually participating in them, and I guess the distance in years between our ages, made us older siblings very protective toward him.

He was deeply loved, so possibly he was always looked upon as a "child", and I for one tried to shield him from many of the more difficult situations – not a good idea perhaps, for he wasn't encouraged to talk about his own opinions, which could have made him feel rather left out. He spent a great deal of his childhood with our grandmother, who undoubtedly gave him the same magical beginning that she gave us all, and later he used to stay with her on week nights as she didn't like sleeping alone after Grandpa died.

So I suppose, apart from playing numerous games of cards at the weekends, and hearing about his football escapades while Dale was locked in his studies, I guess there wasn't much time we younger siblings spent together, for I had left home by the time he was twelve.

Yet it is funny how easy one can be misled and later discover so much in hindsight, for I now know that, in his own way, Keith was far more aware than we gave him credit, and this too, has probably done much to direct his own life.

I always knew he cared very much about people, and was openly generous in nature – especially to the underdog - but I neglected to really appreciate how much he too was affected by events. It is only recently that he has spoken about the past, and says that he used to have terrifying nightmares about the traumas that occurred in the house. Yet he felt he could never tell anyone the real reason, even when he was sent to Great Ormond Street hospital for observation because of his dreams. Dad was always very concerned that maybe one of us would have the same temperament as Mum, which certainly didn't help our childhood.

Keith has become very much a "loner", like myself. Having founded his own business, and made a really successful career in Advertising Production, working for a number of agencies, he now dedicates most of his retirement to charitable work.

Throughout his studies of the "real" world in Science, Dale never lost his belief in God, but he didn't go to church any more. Neither did I, much beyond my early teens. It bored me to tears. The hymns and the service didn't seem to mean anything anymore - just a ritual of faces, gathering together to talk about each other and their latest scandal. My aunts were good people, and Sheila, my godmother, tried very hard to persevere with her duties, but I think I let her down really.

The only time church meant anything to me was when Gran and I used to sit quietly and alone in the old pews at Footscray, and think about the past and the future and what it all meant. During those times I used to have long conversations with God in my head, and it was then and only then, that some sort of answers seemed to assemble together.

"I've got too used to looking on God as a mate of mine," I said once to Gran. "I just can't think of Him as 'The One' who speaks in a loud voice from burning bushes, or that Jesus was all gentle, meek and mild. He would have had to have been a very forceful character or He wouldn't have survived."

"Well, He didn't, did He, dear?" Gran said logically. She patted my hand, as was her way.

"Well, they tell us He did. Oh, you know what I mean!" I had caught her smiling at me. "The Bible is so full of contradictions. One minute God is supposed to be loving and forgiving of all things, and the next minute He is raving like a lunatic out of a cloud. How are we supposed to make sense of that?"

"It's no different from life you know," she said wisely. "The Bible is just a picture book of life. Very few people really understand it. That's why it's such a clever book. It has answers in it for everyone. It's just a question of interpretation. The scientists speak to us only of facts, and the priests only of faith. They're just trying to say the same thing really."

"Yes, that's just it. Reality and imagination can't be that far apart. Surely there must be a meeting point somewhere that is right for everyone?" I said.

51

"Undoubtedly there is," she replied. "And undoubtedly it's very simple, but the problem we all seem to face, is trying to find out where one ends and the other begins."

7 CHASING GHOSTS

I left home and school at sixteen years old. My mother's illness had become very disruptive to my studies and, being the only girl, it was expected in the 1950's that I should take time off to look after the family. This filled me with irritation because I was never born to natural domesticity, and resented the fact that I was required to carry out the most boring of chores. Besides, Dale kept interfering by turning down the gas jets without telling me, and ridiculing my inability to make decent custard. He was right of course.

Anyway, my father suggested that it would be better if both Dale and I left home around the same time, to make things easier for Mum. She still seemed to find us very difficult when she was not in hospital, and as my brother was now eighteen and going to university it seemed the expedient thing to do.

I didn't mind at all, in fact it was a great relief to be moving away from all the conflict.

My mother was born in the 1st world war and I was born in the 2nd. Mum's mother died when she was ten years old - the same age as I was when she herself became so ill – and she ran away from home at sixteen years old - exactly the same age as I was then. My birthday was also the same day as my mother's sister, Aunt Joan. It all seemed a little strange, and I did wonder if events were more than a co-incidence at the time. Later I recalled this again, when other chance happenings seemed to occur.

However, for the time being I was full of excitement. Shortly afterwards I found a job in London, and went to live in a flat with four other girls in the centre of town. Those were a few years of great happiness, laughter and love affairs. I seem to remember I very rarely had any money or ever slept. There was too much to do and experience, and the freedom was an absolute dream to enjoy.

There was a very dear friend called Eric, whom I had known since my early school days, and now lived close by our place, in a tumbledown, damp ridden room off Kensington High Street. We spent a lot of time together, sharing the poverty and bright lights of London. I used to defend him from his girlfriends, and he'd support me through all the devastating consequences of the men in my life, for I was never one to do anything by halves and was often getting caught in horrendous situations from which he felt obliged to extricate me.

Eric was the first of the truly great loves of my life. Somebody who held a quality that bound me inexplicably to him like an unseen hand. He used to protect me like a father and love me like a brother, but never were we lovers in all the long years we've known each other. Even before we became friends we seemed to know each other and what we thought and felt, as if somehow we'd been through it all before. I tried to analyse it once in my usual questioning way, but he quietened me by saying,

"It's enough to know that things are as they are. To question too much is to break into the privacy of a dream, and a broken dream is the prelude to disillusionment. Leave things as they are."

It was odd though how we seemed to do everything together. We even got married only two weeks apart. He fell in love with a black-eyed French beauty called Danielle, with a genius for interior design, and I married Adrian, a public school boy with brilliance for sport.

The four of us were inseparable for a long while, and between us we had four children, born very much at the same time. They were all extremely boisterous. Ours were blonde with blue eyes, named Simon and Matthew, and theirs were dark with brown eyes, named Mark and Luke. I never appreciated how funny this was until I was running down Hampstead High Street one day, trying to contain them all and yelling,

"Matthew, Mark, Luke, Simon – WAIT!"

A woman at a nearby bus stop sniffed loudly, and observed to her friend,   "She's got the whole bleeding Bible there. It will be John and Jesus next."

****

During those few years in London, and up until my marriage, I became obsessed by the investigation of psychology. I probably read a great number of books, but nothing, no matter how hard I tried to change my viewpoint, gave me a satisfactory answer to the problem of finding the thin dividing line between imagination and reality. Everything I read talked about the "power of the mind", but not how to contain it, or what made the difference between one person's truth and another person's falsehood. However, since I was still just a teenager and so full of intensity, it's very likely I overlooked some significant points at the time.

It was frustrating that - although my father was then an authority on the Christian religion, and made a study of many others; whilst Dale was deeply involved in the physics, and I had immersed myself in psychology - we still didn't seem to be able to come up with a common answer that successfully aligned with the "truth" I was struggling to find. Of course it was helpful in its way, and certainly gave a more rounded view of the world, but there were so many opposing opinions; each one seemingly designed to outcast the other.

The apparent impossibility of finding any form of conclusion was greatly upsetting. Wanting so badly to find an answer to the torment my mother had been suffering, in my youthful ignorance I had launched into the fray without thought of the reality of such an involvement.

"You know why that is?" Eric said one day, when I felt I was going to blow up with frustration and confusion.

"Why?" I asked, holding my head in my hands, and trying to relieve the pressure on my neck.

"It's because you are searching for the meaning of life, not only a cure for mental illness. You'll do yourself in if you're not careful. You'll never find a satisfactory solution that way. Philosophy is probably the best subject to study. We just have to accept that logic and fantasy don't mix, and never will do."

"But they must do somewhere" I replied vehemently. "There's got to be a common denominator, or at least a bridge that can take us from one side to the other without losing our sanity in the process" I paused suddenly, as a thought struck me ...

"And what about the psychics and clairvoyants – those who deal in the paranormal? Where do they fit into all this? The way things are it is impossible for them to communicate with the mathematicians of the world without being ridiculed out of existence. And don't tell me that all those people who believe in these things are crackers. It's just not possible for all of them to be wrong."

"I'm not saying a word." Eric stared at me with a deadpan face - taking on the look of the comedienne Marty Feldman in his hilarious silent films. He didn't have the same protruding eyes, but there was definitely a likeness, and it always made me laugh. He smiled and continued wisely,

"Well, you've given science, religion and psychology a hammering, how about giving ghosts, visions and clairvoyants a chance?   But remember one thing, no one person can change the world."

"I wouldn't presume to try!"

"Want a bet?" He laughed.

And so it was, that I threw myself head first into half the Spiritualist Churches in London. If any of these poor people had got wind of my coming they would have been wise to close their doors and run but, in their innocence, they welcomed me with open arms, and suffered the onslaught of many an impossible question for their pains.

The thing that frustrated me most was that there seemed to be even less answers from there, than I had gleaned from anywhere else. All I got for my arrogance was "knowing" smiles and patient silence, but no explanations that I could grab hold of.

Looking back, it was obvious why, for I had plummeted straight into the midst of illusion and expected to find facts. A further disadvantage was that these people had no understanding as to why it was all so important, and they seemed to run out of energy when trying to explain. A friendly white haired old woman, enveloped in an over large kaftan, epitomised it for everyone else, by saying,

"My dear child, you're not *ready* to know. When you *are*, it will all become clear."   At the time I was very irritated, and dismissed her as a doddering idiot.

"I wish they wouldn't keep smiling patiently at me," I complained loudly to Eric. "They obviously think they know something I don't, and I have to constantly resist the urge to wop them."

"Have you tried listening?" he asked annoyingly.

"What do you mean, have I tried listening? I'm always listening. They just talk gobble de gook, and float around two feet off the ground, like unfulfilled priests."

"Well, that's an achievement in itself"

"I'm serious, Eric!" I scowled at him in frustration.

"I know," he said. "That's probably half the trouble. You're far too intense. How can anyone explain anything successfully to someone who is staring into their faces with piercing concentration, and trying to catch them out in every other sentence? To become an authority on any subject you have to first learn its language. Even science and religion have a language of their own that has to be learned in order to understand. How about *listening* first and asking questions later?"

"But I am trying to listen," I argued. "I've learned that the Aura is a luminous field of force that surrounds the body of all things, but I've never seen one. I've sat in circles and talked to people that are known to be dead, but never once have I touched one. What more can I do? It's stupid if you aren't allowed to put something to the test."

"That's just it," Eric remarked, "your form of test is to grab a ghost by the throat and shake it into reality. But you've got to *see* one first before you can catch it"

"So what am I supposed to do?"

"Heaven knows! Perhaps you need to buy some glasses."

So I took his advice, and tried to stop asking questions and listen more. In many ways I learned a great deal about the "theory" behind the belief in psychic phenomena, but still there seemed to be nothing tangible that didn't rely on a lot of gullibility and a great deal of faith.

It wasn't that I didn't believe in it. It would have been easier to dismiss it as pure garbage, but there were too many vague truths for that. It was just that the gulf between fact and fantasy seemed to get wider instead of narrower. Finally, I became bored with continuous conversations with invisible beings, which seemed to lead precisely nowhere, and faded off the scene.

****

So, at 20 years old, I had roared into marriage, and would move out again seven years later. In the mean time I produced two boy children whom I loved dearly, but nearly drove me completely up the wall. If ever Dale and I were always at loggerheads, Simon and Matthew seemed to be worse. But then I was the mother this time. It was like being in charge of two wild buck rabbits, continually rolling around the floor and teasing each other endlessly, especially in shops, which always left people scowling at me as if I had brought them out especially to disrupt the world.

With only 15 months between my two boys, I found it very hard to keep them amused, but once I was lucky and found some workmen digging up the road during a dismal winter. Peace reigned, for they seemed to really enjoy watching them, so I used to take them there every day, which kept them quiet for a while. However, I was sharply disillusioned when one day we were late home, and I hurried us all past the end of the road. Simon suddenly grabbed hold of his brother and pulled him along urgently, saying in a low confidential tone,

"Quick, don't let mummy see those men, or we will

be here for ages!"

Another time, I trudged them dutifully to the park in the rain, and fell flat on my face as I slipped in the mud. I scrambled hurriedly to my feet only to see both of them staring with bemused faces, before walking coolly on, leaving me trailing behind. Simon put a comforting arm round his brother, saying casually,

"Isn't Mummy silly sometimes?"

These were only a couple of incidents out of many that occurred, and they led me to ponder the possibility of Simon taking over Dale's role as the Wisest Owl in the book – a position I can proudly say, he has now certainly fulfilled!

In those early days I can't say I was a good mother, for I was far too covetous of my lost freedom. Having been brought up in such different circumstances, I found what was expected of a 'normal' mother, quite alien. Unfortunately, Adrian didn't really help the situation, for he came from a world that expected the wife to automatically take on these feminine duties with ease. Nevertheless, I did try hard to conform to the necessary protocol, but found it both bewildering and overwhelming, and ended up going through a terribly neurotic phase, where I was continually fed up and sorry for myself.

So, far from progressing towards a possible solution to my mother's problem, I tried to shut it completely from my mind. Having nearly blasted my head off throughout the years of my teens, I gave the whole lot up as a complete waste of time, and sank into the mundane routine of family life, which seemed to fluctuate from exhaustion to boredom.

Yet in spite of this rather fatalistic and dramatic decision, the world has a way of moving a person steadily forward, aiming at a goal that only sometimes becomes clear in retrospect. During those strange and confusing years of my youth I began, unknowingly, to piece together vital information, and learned two very important principles through my parents that were to be of great value in later life.

8 MY PARENT'S LEGACY

It was very early in my marriage that my father gave me a profound answer to something, which stays with me today. It was a valuable lesson in objectivity, and seeing things from a different angle when caught amidst the problem of self-pity. I wasn't a person who found it particularly hard to be decisive but when faced with traumatic incidents it is often difficult to be objective, and I was far too emotional then.

I caught German measles, when just pregnant with my first child. Because of the risks involved, it was advised to have the pregnancy terminated, which led to all sorts of horrific consequences in my mind. I went through a massive confrontation of conscience - my spiritual upbringing versus the strong possibility of a blind, deformed or mentally retarded child. It was the latter of these that capped it for me and, although the decision was made to follow the doctor's advice I just couldn't come to terms with it.

What made it worse was that my mother became obsessively upset and demanded to visit me just after the event. She created a dramatic confrontation in the hospital, for she insisted I was terribly wrong to 'kill that baby' – as she put it – and warned me that I would regret it forever. This left me feeling utterly bereft and - because it was too late - I was totally overcome with remorse and grief.

"I never do anything nasty to anyone," I complained to my father. "Neither do any of us, yet we all have such a bad time. What's wrong with our family?" My father looked at me for a minute before walking over to a picture and, taking it down from the wall, he placed it in front of me.

"Do you like that picture, dear?"

"Yes, you know I do." It was photo of the old

Doomsday Church in Footscray that I had copied sometime in my early teens.

"Why?"

"Well, I don't know. I just do."

"Do you think it would be as nice if it was painted all white?"

"Of course not! It wouldn't be a picture then."

"Right, so imagine for a minute that this picture is an image of life here on earth, and we are only a speck of paint in it." He pointed to a dismal, muddy section that looked dark and uninviting. I hadn't really noticed it before. "Perhaps our job in life is to be a speck of paint in this ditch. It might not look very pretty on it's own, but it helps shape the picture, and if someone was to put a blob of light paint there instead, it would wreck the whole impression wouldn't it?"

"Well yes, I suppose so." I said. "But why should anyone be forced to be part of a ditch and someone else allowed to be part of a flower?"

"I can't answer that dear. Maybe it's the luck of the draw."

"Well, that's not fair!"

"Maybe it isn't, but if we're only a minute section of the picture of existence, we're hardly in a position to judge what's fair."

"So, we just have to accept it?"

"Perhaps, and then perhaps not."

"What does that mean?"

My father smiled,

"In every set of circumstances there's *always* a choice. Every sweep of a paintbrush has a chance of changing the artist's original decision. When we're caught in what seems like an impossible situation, we should ask ourselves one question – *'Can I stand this or can't I?'* - If the answer is *'No',* then we should investigate how we can *change* things, but if we *can't* change it, then it's no use bemoaning our fate. We have to learn to live *with* it. And the best way to live with it is to *change our attitude* – not the situation - and try to get some pleasure out of what we've got."

·I was silent for I knew he was right, but it was a tall order to ask of anyone when they were in the depths of despair. Perhaps we were such a minute part, that we'd never be able to see the overall picture, but, even so, surely we should be allowed to know why we were put into the section we were in?

"But I still don't see why The Creator would make such choices. There must be reasons?"

"Indeed there must be" Dad smiled, "But these are things that none of us will probably ever know."

****

Another vital lesson for not taking everything at face value – even when you think you know it all - was shown by my mother, who, in spite of her illness, was a person of great intelligence and profound awareness that often remained hidden, due to her problems..

We all tended to categorise her as someone who needed 'special attention' like an invalid, and tried in our own way to humour her through the variance of her moods, for quite often this helped to avoid the full violence of her temper. However, I am not sure that we were very sensitive to her other needs - like considering whether she had a sense of humour, or could really appreciate what was going on around her.

She was rarely involved in everyday conversations or circumstances - or at least, I think we fell into the habit of not involving her perhaps.

My marriage took me some distance away from my parents, and I didn't see much of them, but when Adrian went on a business trip, and the children were being looked after by their other grandparents, I felt it was a reasonable idea to have my mother to stay. It was during one of her 'better times', and as those were rare, it seemed a good chance to try and do something together.

While she was staying, we had decided to re-cover the lounge suite as Mum was a genius with the needle, and I knew this would make her happy to concentrate on more pleasurable things. It would be great to see if we could spend some quality time together for once.

When the appointed day arrived, Mum and Dad duly appeared, loaded up with a vast old sewing machine and reams of patterns and threads etc., all packed in the boot of the car. Dad stayed for a cup of tea, and then moved on, as he had a long journey ahead.

Eager to get on, Mum and I settled down to start work. However, having set everything up and begun to cut out the pattern, we found that the sewing 'foot' of the machine was missing, and it was impossible to do without it.

"It must have dropped off in the boot of the car," observed Mum. "I'll phone Keith, and tell him to ask Dad to put it in the post when he gets back."

"Keith? Hello dear, we've just arrived and....yes, it was a good journey. Now listen. Tell your father when he gets home that I've lost the 'foot' of the machine in the boot of the car... What? ... No, the FOOT, dear! It's in the boot. And can he post it on to us, or we won't be able to get started. Yes, dear, I said the FOOT."

It must have been an hour later when the phone rang. I answered it unsuspectingly.

"What on earth is going on down there?" My father's voice boomed out loudly.

"Nothing, why?"

"Well what's all this about me having to post your mother's foot in my boot?"

Realisation dawned, and I burst out laughing, which wasn't greatly appreciated by my father at first.

"I can't understand it," he muttered. "She seemed quite well when I left a couple of hours ago. Do you want me to come and pick her up?"

After much explanation, and a lot of waving of arms and chortles at my end, I put down the phone to find my mother sat on the end of the settee, crumpled in a heap with tears running down her face. My immediate reaction was alarm, until the shaking silence burst open with peals of laughter, which lasted for a full few minutes with both of us rolling around everywhere.

"Facts are said to be stranger than fantasy!" she gasped after a while. "There you all are, thinking *I'm* loony, and I look at you, wondering where on earth the difference is!"

"Oh, Mum!" I felt terribly ashamed. I wasn't sure that she was really aware of what went on in our day-to-day lives. She stopped laughing suddenly, and looked at me seriously,

"There isn't much to tell the difference between us all," she said "I know that I have worries that may, or may not be true. Often I don't know which is which - or so I'm told - but I'm not a fool you know and I don't have

66

to be treated like a fool. I know what's going on sometimes better than those who think they know.

"There is a woman I met in the hospital who thought that the doll she was holding was a child - her child - the one that died. She named her with same name and everything. You can't blame her for imagining things. That doll was real to her – a living thing. Sometimes it helps the pain to imagine. I understand these things. I'm not a fool, but they don't see that..." She seemed to dismiss the subject and went back to her sewing.

I felt very despondent, for here was my mother, who was saying things that I couldn't dispute, yet I also knew that when she was at her worst there was no such interaction of understanding between herself and others - just an obsession with the subject that was the nearest to her pain - and there was no way to discuss anything with her then.

Again I found myself wondering where the line was between the two worlds of reality. There were so many dividing lines. Would they ever end? My mother had been shoved into a box and categorised, not only by the doctors, but also her family. And it was because we had failed to find the dividing line that she remained on drugs - for that was the safest way - the only way for those who had to cope with her. Yet, I still couldn't believe it was right.

I watched her as she started pinning the pattern onto the material. Her face was deep in concentration, but I could see the futility and underlying grief etched in her eyes. She glanced up suddenly, as if expecting me to ask a question. The tears of her recent laughter still lingered on her cheek, making her sorrow seem all the more poignant, and I felt she was holding on to some terrible inner secret that she couldn't find the words to express. I tried earnestly to talk to her while I could.

"Mum, why can't you just laugh at your worries and

what other people think?" I ventured, thinking yet again of Gran, her 'Make Believe', and her purple hat. She was silent for a long time. Then she said, as though to a child,

"Would *you* be able to laugh when you're sobbing from the soles of your feet? Would *you* be able to laugh when you're telling the truth and the doctors decide you're making it up? I don't trust doctors. They sometimes do the wrong things and people die! It's all very well for everyone to judge, but they don't really know the truth - see what I've seen, and hear what I've heard – they're not in my position." She stopped abruptly, as if not wanting to talk about it anymore.

I waited in silence, wishing so much to continue the conversation: to find out what it was that she was trying to say, but she made it quite obvious that the subject was closed.   What were these 'things' that were haunting her so badly? Were they just stories, or did they really happen? And who would ever believe her anyway?

I felt ashamed for my lack of awareness, for my mother had sharply reminded me of one very important point I had somehow forgotten - like any other human being, she was still capable of change and objective thought, as well as laughter.

As I sat beside her, I was mortified that I was completely unable to do anything realistic to help her. You see, in the old days there wasn't so much understanding of my mother's condition as there is today.   People like her, diagnosed with paranoid schizophrenia, were an embarrassment to the public and locked away - sometimes for life.   And people like us – her family - were not enlightened by the doctors, who seemed to know little themselves, so we had to fight through a mire of confusion to even begin to make any sense of it all.

And what I find more saddening is - that even now as I write this over 60 years later - there appears little evidence of advance in treatments, and we are still often left with no alternative but, in the opinion of most of the medical profession, to keep the patient on drugs.

It was only much later that I found out the real truth of my mother's heartbreak and subsequent breakdown. If attitudes towards the emotional welfare of people in the 1950s severely lacked understanding then, how much harder it must have been for her, born in 1917 in the latter days of the first Great War, and left to face a responsibility too great for a young child to bear.

9 ALL THINGS BEING EQUAL

Life continued to move on, and so did the world around us. My dearly beloved grandmother died at a ripe old age, and, although deeply missed, left behind a host of happy memories that remain as an everlasting influence with all of us.   Certainly, I will always remember her as someone who enriched the world with the kind of magic that I fear we have now lost to a long forgotten era.

I was the first to marry, but soon Dale met a lovely girl at university named Viv, and they took the plunge shortly after. I think she was his first love, and was probably his saviour, for without her I doubt if he would have become such a well-balanced and happy family man as he is today.

Keith had grown up too. He remained living at home for a long time, but followed me into advertising, and at 27 years founded "Tapestry Colour" - his own very successful business.

Seven years passed, and Adrian and I grew apart. We married very young, and sadly found we had little in common as we became older. So eventually we decided to call it a day. I was probably far too dramatic and unconventional for Adrian and his family - for they were the breed of the "stiff upper lip" and "old boys" in pubs, which sometimes put me at loggerheads with my mother in-law in particular. She disliked the fact that I went bra-less whenever I could, and didn't quite live up to the "class" she tried to represent.

Coming from the intensity and all encompassing approach of my background, I disliked snobbery of any kind, and resented having to demurely attend the marathon of golf clubs and superficial cocktail parties, whilst only being able to express ideas that neatly conformed to the role of a dutiful wife. Opinionated as it probably was, I felt the whole way of life was devoid of any real depth of feeling, and certainly wasn't for me.

Because I had moved such a distance from my hometown, and was now occupied in bringing up two very young children as a single mother, I saw less and less of my family. Coupled with that, Mum's problems seemed to worsen again after Dale had Paul, his first child. It was difficult to know why. Anyway, Dad and I had always felt it best that, because of Mum's health, Simon and Matthew should only stay when he was at home. It was because of this, and the long distance away, the visits became very rare events.

Over the following year I started to think more and more of my mother's family and what, if anything, her upbringing had done to affect her life. She had one sister called Joan; a half sister "Little Doris", and stepmother Doris that Mum obviously loathed; plus a father who seemed to have a rather large ego and was more interested in his scientific pursuits than his family.

Joan had exactly the same birth date as mine, which was very distressing and significant to Mum, although I didn't know why then.

There was also a strange but very beautiful great aunt Eugenie – sister of my grandmother - and her husband, who sported the oddest name Athol, and professed to have a special affinity with tigers. He had immensely long arms that made him look a bit like a friendly ape from behind. They both seemed much more orientated to Italian royal breeding and the colonial world of India, than our British heritage.

As for my Grandfather, I never got to know him, for he seemed totally indifferent to us, and always made himself scarce when we were around. Besides, his very presence in the household seemed to arouse acute tension, which often led to the inevitable rows between my mother, Joan and their stepmother. The sad thing is that I didn't even remember his name until Dale told me recently it was Bill – funny to have two grandparents called Bill or William, and how different they were in attitude.

By all accounts Mum's father was a brilliant man, who had once been a very wealthy "inventor" or something, who spent much of his time abroad, as well as having his own laboratory in Scotland. I remember him as an arrogant, dour, old man, with a large square head accentuated by a shock of grey hair: two fingers missing from his right hand, and an alarming looking twitch in his eye. He lost his fingers whilst working on an early motorbike. The story goes that my grandmother was back in India at the time, but had one of her "visions", and warned him rather dramatically by telegram, but he took no notice - as was his way – and whilst he was cleaning between the spokes of a wheel, the gardener started up the engine.

We very rarely went to see Mum's family. The few times we did go, there always seemed to be huge commotions about the past. I remember Joan cried a lot - especially when their mother, was mentioned - and Mum got far too upset and cross. The most I gleaned from these encounters was that my Italian grandmother came from royalty; was very psychic, extremely highly strung, and a brilliant musician who died in strange circumstances when my mother was only ten years old. Many times in the midst of the quarrels, Dad used to get really fed-up and hustle us all away as fast as possible, which normally put the rest of the week into utter turmoil.

The more I thought about this, and the extreme differences in "Fate" that appeared in life, the more I questioned my father's belief in the "Bigger Picture", for it still seemed to be so terribly unfair.

Having been brought up as a Christian, I had been taught to believe that there was only one life, and our only experience was the one we were born into. If we were good, we went to heaven and if we were bad, we went to hell. But, try as I would, I couldn't come to terms with the thought that our whole fate and fortune was determined by the whim of an intangible Force.

I was forever querying the reasoning behind the continuous suffering of some and the lack of suffering of others. It also seemed a terrifying thought, that we could lead what we might consider, 'very good lives', only to find, that after death, a jumbo finger was pushing us steadfastly through the gates of eternal damnation without giving us the chance to understand why.

It was whilst struggling with this dilemma that I found myself caught up in the deeply exciting and fascinating theory of 'Karma'.

In those days it really *was* just the beginning of the so-called "enlightened" age, and these sorts of subjects were far from being overt in the literary sense. So when I discovered a book on re-incarnation - belief in many lives - I was completely overwhelmed and read it with increasing interest and enthusiasm. It was the first time in all those years of questions that I felt I'd come across some semblance of an answer without having to drive myself, or others, demented in the process.

I found to my excitement, that the idea of karma gave me feasible answers to so many questions, for this way of living could be termed as a massive school of continuous learning, each life reacting to, and compensating for, the errors and achievements made in previous existences.

It was when I was trying to explain this theory to yet another scientific brain box - whose name escapes me, but I had found at a party - that I made a connection that was to become a major turning point in my life.

"So what's Karma?" he asked, after listening sceptically to me rabbiting on about many lives for some while. "It's always the same with people who philosophise over things. They talk for hours and never explain anything. If we're supposed to believe in something, it's got to have a purpose and I don't see the purpose."

"If you'd listen, I'm explaining it!" I announced in frustration.

"Not very clearly," he said. "So if reincarnation means many lives, what's Karma?"

"Karma is the *result* of our behaviour in previous lives. It's like a debt we pay off, or a gift we receive."

"Oh," he sounded dangerously near boredom. I struggled for simplicity.

"Listen! Everything is in cycles, just like the seasons. We chop up a year into lots of days don't we - and days into hours? So why not chop up one massive life or experience into lots of little lives or experiences? If you get too drunk tonight, you'll pay the price with a hangover tomorrow won't you? That's Karma. It's a direct result of what we've done before; only this belief extends further and goes from lifetime to lifetime, instead of day to day".

I paused, waiting for a reaction, but he didn't say anything, so I continued stubbornly,

"*Now* do you see? It makes sense of so many things, particularly why some people seem to have so much suffering and others have none at all. It's not God's choice - it's ours. We have to learn to adjust to attain perfection. What we have sown, even the Bible says that we reap."

"Every action has an equal and opposite reaction,"

he muttered.

"What?"

"I said, every action has an equal and opposite reaction," he repeated. "It's called the Law of Cause and Effect."

"What?"

"Goodness! Do you mean to tell me you've never heard of it? Surely you know about Newton?" The guy looked at me incredulously. "I don't believe it! Here you are spouting all about Karma being a direct result of previous action, and you've never heard of Newton's third law of motion. For your information, Newton proved that forces react to each other."

"*So?*"

"Well, it's like the wiring of an electrical plug. There is a positive force and an equal negative force, which react against each other. When this doesn't happen it becomes out of balance, and nothing works – which means no electricity and therefore no lights! But if there is too much reaction from one side or the other, it blows a fuse. See? You ought to look around you more. Everything reacts to each other.*"*

"So this can apply to humans as well?

"Perhaps. Any form of over reaction is just the same as blowing a fuse. Every action has an equal and opposite reaction. It's the perfect balance we seek in science - and in nature come to that. The world is in continual adjustment and re-adjustment. It's a pity human beings don't seem to do the same. They're forever over reacting to everything and causing chaos."

"Oh but they *do* adjust! They do! That's just what I've been saying. Surely that's what Karma is all about? If we act badly, then we get an equal return of difficulty later in life or in the next! And if we act well it's visa versa. Wow! I can't believe it. Do you realise what you've just told me?"

"What?"

"That the parable of the Scattering of Seeds and the Law of Cause and Effect are one and the same thing! We reap what we sow. Science has actually proved what the Bible has said all along."

"I never said that. It's you who are saying that. All I said was that you talking about Karma reminded me of the Law of Cause and Effect. Anyway, the Bible doesn't advocate reincarnation...."

"But they are the same thing. Newton's theory, the Karmic theory and the Bible's theory - they're all the same, but just said in a different language. Eric was right, every subject speaks in a different language."

"Who's Eric?"

"Oh, he's a friend. I talk a lot to him."

"Poor Eric," he commiserated with himself.

I fell silent for a moment, lost in excitement at having stumbled across what seemed in my ignorance a direct link that united both fact and faith. If Science and Religion had one statement in common, there must be others. Then a puzzling thought crossed my mind.

"I was just wondering..." I hesitated. "I was just wondering... if every action has an equal and opposite reaction...how would the first action have started in the beginning?"

The poor guy raised his hands in a gesture of hopelessness. *"God knows!"* he said, and was obviously right!

10 WHO SAYS WHAT?

For some weeks after that, I spent hours pouring over everything I could find to do with science and particularly any form of religion. Looking back, it was quite obvious that I wouldn't find anything conclusive, for I was looking in too many places at once. Coupled with that, being completely ignorant in scientific realms, I would have to rely on other people for interpretation.

The books were useless to me, for I had absolutely no idea where to begin, and kept finding obscure information which meant precisely nothing. It seemed that the language of science was as brain shattering as the language of the psychic was utterly confusing.

You may wonder why this obsessive study was so important to me, and why, from the beginning, I tried to pursue the different revelations with such logical vengeance. All I can say is that it seemed vital at the time, if only to challenge my own disbelief by confirming the authenticity of other more secret and hidden worlds.

Having been brought up strongly flanked by the realism of my brother and father, it seemed ridiculous - in the face of my mother's illness - to place too much accent on instinctive feelings and imagination without at least starting from a solid foundation of reason. When trying to break new ground in the approach to mental health, it became very clear that simple faith and belief were not enough to sustain the interest of the sceptic.

I am glad that I approached it that way, for all these things certainly grew in significance as time went on. In fact, one seemingly chance encounter, led me to discover an aspect of the Jewish Religion, which became fundamental in explanation for me - not only in understanding of our physical and universal worlds, but that of the emotional, mental, and spiritual complexities of the mind.

By now I was more than convinced that the philosophy of Karma was a truth that could well be linked with another time, and place - yet the dimension we lived in was so small by comparison with the whole, it surely was impossible to see or understand it all in one cycle of experience?

It was easy to see now that "The Bigger Picture" described by my father, was both just and fair. There would be continual change and readjustment to the picture according to the status of each individual within it.

So it was clear that there *was* a reason for events and circumstance, and that reason was directly as a result of our own involvements in the past. We were responsible for ourselves; and were being taught, not on a whim, but for the purpose of learning from experience, just as children learn only from experience. This process of growth, to my mind, had to span a far greater period than one short life - otherwise what was the ultimate purpose? Where did it lead us?

However, at this moment in time, there was one important question that I just couldn't resolve.

Why did many religions believe in reincarnation and not Christianity?

With my background I was very hesitant to challenge any religious concepts, but this question would just not go away, and before I knew it I found myself confronting an innocent man in a dog collar whom I found in Chichester Cathedral. Adrian and I had moved close to Portsmouth in the last year of our marriage and I had driven over there one afternoon,

"Do you think Christ believed in reincarnation?" I asked.

The man remained silent. In fact, I began to wonder

if he'd become a pillar of stone, but he must have been thinking, for he turned politely, with a look of amazement on his face.

"Well, what makes you ask a question like that?"

"Ye shall reap as ye have sown."

"Yes?"

"It's the parable of the scattering of the seeds."

"Yes?"

He was obviously waiting, so I explained things as carefully and as clearly as I could, but he wouldn't agree, any more than anyone else. It was all such a nuisance.

"I don't really think that Jesus meant that," he said finally.

"Well, what *did* He mean then?"

"Well... He meant that we should do good things in life or we won't reap the rewards in future... " He seemed to fade out.

"In other words, don't sow weeds if you want to grow roses?"

"Well, yes!" He laughed.

"So surely that's just what I'm saying! The only difference is that I'm talking about a longer time span. Karma applies to this life, or it can apply to many lives?" He was silent for what seemed like ages,

"I don't know about karma or re-incarnation," he said finally. "And if the Good Lord wanted us to know about it, He would have told us."

Well, what can you answer to that? I wanted to yell in a huge voice that the Good Lord WAS telling us, but we weren't listening! It was all there in the Bible for everyone to see, *'Do unto others as you would have them do unto you'.* What did that mean then, if it wasn't the Law of Cause and Effect?

I stopped, for quite suddenly I heard the distant voice of my grandmother whispering in my ear.

'It's just a question of interpretation, dear. The Bible is such a clever book. It has answers in it for everyone."

I thanked him, and rather sullenly took my leave.

"It's no good," I thought, as I stubbornly walked up the road, "Eric as always, is right. I've forgotten to listen again, and by talking too much, I've probably frightened the answers into silence." Yet I suspected the poor man didn't have any answers at all, and I had just succeeded in irritating him with a seemingly nonsensical idea.

****

It's an extraordinary thing but, often when searching for something in one place, it's found in another. I don't know what made me walk into a bookshop in Golders Green the next time I was in London. It seemed so old and musty, and there was an ancient Jewish man with a dark greying beard and a skullcap, shuffling behind the counter. I started to wander along the rows of books on the shelves, until I came to the section on religion and began scanning the titles idly.

Still on the 'Karmic' trail, I had by now swung my attention to trying to trace back the history of Christ to His own religious upbringing. He was obviously the founder of the beginnings of Christianity, but He was also a Jew. Maybe if I understood more of the old

Jewish beliefs? I put my hand up to unravel the tattered spine of a book, and it fell with a clatter onto the floor.

Embarrassed, I picked it up and flipped it open, pretending that I had intended to read it. There was a peculiar diagram on the page, which reminded me of some of my brother's experiments, and I was just about to close it in a hurry, when I noticed weird letters underneath, followed by the words, "The Tree of Life." That rang a very loud bell. I turned to the old man at the counter.

"Can you tell me what this book is about?" He shuffled over to me.

"The Kabbalah," he said finally.

"The Kabbalah? What's that?" He peered at me suspiciously before saying,

"You wouldn't be interested unless you understand Hebrew. It's part of the teachings of Judaism."

That did it.

"I'll have it," I said, much to his surprise, but he didn't query, and shoved it into a paper bag. I paid him his money.

"Can I ask you a question?"

He sniffed indifferently, "What?"

"I know Jewish people don't accept the teachings of Christ, but can you tell me why not?" He gave me my change slowly.

"We don't accept he was the Son of God," he said. "It's too long to explain." He turned and busied himself with his papers.

"Thanks." I moved to go but he spoke.

"His teachings were sound enough."

"So you believe He existed?"

"Yes."

I hesitated before saying, "Christ was born a Jew. Surely He was brought up in the Jewish Religion?"

"Perhaps. Why do you want to know?"

"Well...because...I was wondering if the Jews believe in Karma, and if so, then Jesus must have believed in it too...?"

To my embarrassment, the man didn't answer, but just stared at me blankly. There didn't seem much more to say, so I moved to go again.

"Young lady!" He said suddenly. "If you are really interested, make the effort to try to read that book. It's an interpretation of the Old Testament. We believe in the Old Testament, and if your Jesus Christ was truly a Jew, he probably would have known the Kabbalah."

"Thanks." I said, and I tried, really tried, to follow his advice, but I couldn't understand it properly, except in the very superficial sense, for just as he had said, most of it was written in Hebrew, with long bits of translation that did little to hold the attention.

However, I felt there was something very important there, for the Tree of Life was mentioned a great deal, and it seemed to connect with the Biblical Book of Genesis.

So where did that lead me? I had no idea! And off I went again on the continuous road to nowhere.

It was obvious that I was never going to find any

answers to anything, unless I created some order. Yet I was certain in my mind that somewhere amongst all the little pieces of gathered information, there was a continuous line that ran like a tenuous thread through all the branches of science, all the different beliefs of religions, and continued on through fact and fantasy, imagination and reality.

And something was telling me very strongly that there, travelling on that thread - as if straddled across the waters of life - ran the mind and sanity of us all.

Nevertheless, the target I had set myself was too colossal and evasive. If I was ever to be able to do anything of value for my mother or anyone else, it seemed I would have to become an expert on every subject - each of these being so complex, that it had taken far greater brains than my own more than a lifetime to learn. If I continued like this I was indeed putting my own sanity at risk, and at best I could hope for was to find myself a simpleton of all trades and certainly master of none.

I picked up a piece of paper, and started to make headings that might help to co-ordinate all the information discovered so far.

Three hours later I finally put down my pen and looked at the list for a long time. I knew it was futile. Then, slowly and carefully I filed it amongst my notes and, after quietly closing it in a drawer, I sat down and wept.

11 SANDY'S WORLD

After this last experience, I stopped keeping a diary for a while, and tried to move forward with a more relaxed approach. I was severely disillusioned and exhausted by the enormity of the task I had accidentally set myself, and seemed to have completely lost sight of where it was leading. So it was a welcome relief that other lighter events soon took precedence in life.

And yet all the time, the mysteries hidden in my mother's past continued to haunt me in my quieter moments. I never doubted that one-day the secret of her grief, and perhaps cause of her illness, would be revealed. It seemed certain that the two things were intrinsically linked, but also that a door firmly closed whenever the subject was mentioned.

Dad always said he didn't know anything, and suggested that any past upsets were all part of my mother's imagination. However it seemed very odd that when I tried to talk to my aunt Joan about it she would burst into tears, and the rest of her family would just stare sadly and rapidly change the subject. Coupled with that, it was virtually impossible to talk to anyone without my mother being there, which made conversation even more difficult.

And so again time moved on. Like most things in life, there were a series of stepping- stones, with random events and circumstances covertly designed to draw me closer to my ultimate goal. But, regardless of their apparent unimportance at the time, each experience eventually returned my attention to the same objective - finding the common denominator that might perhaps open the hidden doors of the mind.

****

Now, at 27 years old, I had fought to find the answer to life and failed in my marriage. I had two wild youngsters to bring up, who were full of vibrant and explosive energy that needed release. So, in the effort to sustain some form of normality and fun in our lives, we entered a more pleasurable phase, and met some pretty peculiar but wonderfully hilarious people on the way.

Being completely flat broke, it was essential for me to work so I took a job as a barmaid in a beautiful pub in the South of England, and had an amazing time sloshing drinks over anyone who was foolish enough to come within range. I enjoyed those times very much, and it was there I first met Paddy and Sandy.

Paddy was Irish and a policeman - although I'm perfectly sure he never arrested anyone in his life. In fact it always surprised me that he was even considered for the job in the first place. He was probably the most terrifying person to ever sit beside in a car, and he used to 'loon' around all the time, which was hardly conducive to 'law and order' - yet everyone loved him. He wasn't particularly good looking; didn't say much, but 'looked' a lot, and he was one of the funniest people I've ever met.

Those were the days when policemen just had truncheons and whistles, and not everyone was a suspected "terrorist". By the same token 'health and safety' didn't exist, and therefore they weren't required to wear luminous jackets, or form loud shouting 'packs' when arresting fearsome felons. Paddy used to tell me stories of when he was on duty that left me aching with laughter for days afterwards.

Once, when *'traversing the beat through the park'*, he inadvertently sat on the face of a tramp sleeping on a bench. Apparently, the poor fellow woke up and saw him a moment too late and let out a startled yell into his backside. They spent the next two hours feeding each other with cigarettes whilst trying to calm down from the shock.

Another time he kept watch on a house while the owners were away. It was in heavily wooded grounds, and the house was gaunt and dark. One night, he felt very uneasy as he walked up the side path to check the rear doors, and cautiously took out his truncheon to protect himself. Just as he was creeping up to a back window to peer in, he felt a massive crack on the back of his helmet, and swung round to defend himself vigorously, whilst trying to call for assistance.

After a few seconds of flaying arms, obscene words, and a massive grunt as he nearly swallowed his whistle, he found to his amazement that not only was nobody hitting him back, but he was also clutching wildly at thin air. For a moment he was totally bewildered, until another heavy thud by his feet assured him that his violent assailant was only an apple dropping on his head.

As for Sandy, well she was, and still is, an entity all to herself. Rapidly I was to discover that she had an imagination larger than the Houses of Parliament. I would like to say the Universe, but perhaps that is a small exaggeration.

At our first meeting, I didn't take to her at all, and I gather her opinion of me was little higher. I suppose this was to be expected really, for initially we seemed to be two extremes of personality. I was thin, flamboyant and loud, with wild curly hair, electric coloured clothes, and earrings almost down to my waist, whilst Sandy was more olive skinned with a rather Spanish/Italian look about her – mysterious and deeply intense, with long dark tresses pulled back severely into a bow at the nape of her neck. She seemed very nervous, and always wore black.

This just shows how appearances can be deceiving, for in many ways we became mutual saviours to each other. She was heavily pregnant when we first met, but had been abandoned by the father. I was told by a friend that she was having the baby adopted, and badly needed a home. As I also badly needed a lodger, the dye was cast from the beginning. It was difficult at first, but after a week of tense communication, I accidentally threw a piece of toast that hit her on the head, and we suddenly discovered we both had the same sense of humour - which sealed a friendship that has lasted over 44 years.

From the beginning I saw Sandy as someone who is both wide-eyed and innocent, and brings out the protective quality in people she meets. The separation from her son weighed very heavily upon her. So much so that I even suggested he should come to live with us, but unfortunately she had signed the papers for adoption by then, so - in spite of writing a last minute letter - the request was refused.

Every year on his birthday after that, she used to say she felt desperately sad and lonely, although absolutely certain that one day he would find her. And indeed he did – over 30 years later – and I felt so privileged to witness the joy of a reunion that continues today.

Sandy was especially attracted to the psychic fields, but extremely frightened by anything to do with it, which made it somewhat difficult as she was drawn to such things like a moth to a light. This led her into all sorts of obscure and grey areas.

As I have said, her imagination was vast. So huge in fact that often it became reality to her, and yet I was distinctly aware that, although her apparent fantasies were seemingly beyond normal comprehension, she couldn't be termed as bordering on delusional - although I did wonder at times! But then, because her imagination was so wild and vivid, and certainly not backed by reason, I was always wondering what *was* the difference between her sort of visions and the severe lack of reality of the mentally ill?

It all started with the "Dreams". They pervaded her sleep, and often carried on affecting her throughout the day. They were terrible dreams, full of blood, gore and massacre, but for some unaccountable reason her descriptions of them sparked my sense of humour to the point of near hysterics.

I think it was probably the way she re-enacted them with such an intense and alarmed expression on her face. Many is the time that my door was thrown open in the middle of the night, heralding the dramatic entrance of a distraught darker version of "Miss Piggy", flicking back her hair whilst insisting in a huge voice that she had just got lost in a terrible storm and died like a swan in the snow; had seen my feet cut off with a rotary saw, or that she had met a 'Spiv' with jointed wrists, who had poked her in the eye with his walking stick from behind a bush.

I was subjected to many a brilliant screen play, beautifully presented at the foot of my bed, and always I would destroy the whole thing by bursting into convulsive laughter half way through, until she gave up and started to laugh herself. And maybe that was just as well, as it was probably a healthy safety valve, for I was soon to discover that she was an open target for the influence of others, who used to fill her head with stories of terror and disaster that became a source of continual nightmare and dismay.

I had long since been bored by spiritualists, but drawn by Sandy's obvious fascination we went to a few meetings. However, when a glassy eyed man with bush baby hair, came up behind us in a supermarket queue afterwards, staring at her intensely, before remarking *"I recognise you Sister!"* in the loud lyrical voice of a would be priest, she totally freaked out. We never went again.

Sometime later, during one of our mammoth discussions, we then rather stupidly decided that we would hold our own séance at home. In a rash moment, we agreed that we should use an Ouija board, even though I had heard that difficulties could arise from them. It seemed an easy way of doing things and, as always looking for proof, I was intrigued to find out how the whole thing worked. It was indeed a stupid decision.

We arranged a date, and invited a number of friends to join us. Dear old Paddy was amongst them. It started as an exciting night, for we all sat round in gloomy candlelight in the kitchen, whispering, *"Is anybody there?"* in hoarse voices, grinning at each other, until some late-comer tapped on the window and moaned loudly, putting us all in a state of shock.

But then things suddenly started happening. The detail is insignificant, but briefly the glass started to move erratically, spelling out Paddy's name, and that he had been a Monk. We were astounded and highly amused, because Paddy of all people was so unlikely to have been a Monk. We all looked at him and laughed.

"Well, I used to be a Monk," he said simply. Then, pushing his chair back from the table, he got up and started to leave. "I don't think I want to do this anymore. I advise you to leave it alone." He looked very white. We were all absolutely amazed, and too busy discussing to think of carrying on, so eventually everyone wandered home.

Sandy was incredulous at the whole proceedings, and we couldn't believe that it had actually spelled out that information when nobody in the room knew Paddy had been a Monk, and nobody surely could have guessed? There seemed no logical answers, so after a while I gave up, and resolved to put the incident out of my mind.

But Sandy didn't - or, more correctly, she couldn't.

Although by now close friends, we rarely "socialised", so I didn't immediately realise the seriousness, when she started holding the odd session elsewhere with some of her friends. This caused her no end of trouble, with glasses smashing, lights switching off, and any number of weird unaccountable 'happenings' that just compounded her fears.

Poor Sandy, it couldn't be pleasant to see ugly, headless 'beings' suspended in mid-air in the gloom of the night, even if it could be argued that they were a confrontation of fears of her own inner self. Those kinds of horrors could surely knock a person's sanity right off beam?

However, I was later to discover that her dreams and experiences were not all make believe, but the reality of someone with exceptional psychic powers, yet had great difficulty in controlling them.

Inevitably my thoughts turned back to my mother. It was abundantly clear that the psychic powers of some - when not held under control - could bring a certainty to them that might well be dismissed as hallucination by others. But were the terrors induced, brought about by a terrible fear of the unknown? Surely the influence of others could have a devastating effect on the minds of the credulous?

So there it was. The whole experience had just given weight to yet another burning question.

What was the difference between my mother and Sandy, and was there really much difference between mental illness and psychic trauma?

12 THE "BABY"

The more time I spent with Sandy, the more I felt she should meet my family. When I told her stories about my upbringing, she was very sympathetic with my mother's situation, and even stated that she felt she already knew her. Possibly because her own father was a nurse in a mental hospital, she seemed to have a strong affinity and insight into Mum's illness. It was therefore inevitable that we would soon arrange a meeting.

We planned a weekday as someone could pick up Simon and Matthew from school. My father and Keith were at work, so it would only be the three of us. It was not the normal arrangement, for I missed my father, and things were always easier when he or my brother were around. However, it was obviously "meant to be", for at that meeting a very strange thing happened.

We arrived early. It was one of those balmy spring days, and the world was bright. My parents lived in a leafy London suburb. The road looked beautiful with the trees in flower, and the grass at the edge of the pavement alive with green.

Our family home was built in the '30's - a wedding gift from my father's parents. I think it was new at the time, for it certainly looked in the style of that era, with its' square fronted bay, leaded glass windows, and deep open porch. There was a driveway to the garage that stood next to the side gate by the house; a small square lawn surrounded by shrubbery and flowers at the front, with a low gate and a crazy paving path leading up to the entrance.

My mother loved the garden, and seemed to find some solace in tending to it. When we were young she made a rockery in the front area that she filled with glistening stones – many of which looked as if they were slowly forming into crystals. As we walked up the path, Sandy noticed them immediately, enthralled by their sparkle in the sunlight, and we stood for a while admiring their brilliance. I glanced up and saw Mum watching us through the window; with some relief I took this as a signal that she hadn't forgotten we were coming.

It was the family custom to go through the side gate and into the house by the back door, but it was locked, so we returned to the front and knocked. Nobody came, and for a moment I thought Mum was refusing to answer, but suddenly the door opened and there she was, dressed to receive guests, smiling as if all things in the world were good.

Sandy, as usual, was dressed in black, with her long dark hair tied back as normal. She and my mother smiled politely at each other as we moved into the dining room where the table was laid with a multitude of cakes and sandwiches.

Most of the furniture in the room was made of dark wood that had been hand carved by an uncle of my father's. The dresser with its' spiral struts and heavy intricate design was a masterpiece in itself, but I don't think any of us were too overwhelmed by its beauty. It was very Victorian in style.

Anyway, Mum was an excellent cook, and, in her better times, she always welcomed people with a copious amount of food and drink. And so the day started by eating and drinking, with gentle, superficial conversation. I was very relieved that the atmosphere seemed quite relaxed, for afterwards Sandy was proudly shown round the back garden, talking and smiling with my mother as they looked into the old summer house of childhood memories, and enthused over the rhubarb that had grown giant over the years in the vegetable patch behind.

I watched them through the French doors as I sat in the dining room, noticing Sandy's admiring expression as she was introduced to the arched wooden frames covered in roses, standing along the front edge of the lawn behind the house, and her animation as she got into a heavy discussion concerning the pros and cons of when to prune the huge Buddleia bush to the right of the open doors. I was glad we had come, for they were talking together like old friends.

It was only when they returned, and we all moved into the lounge, that I became aware that my mother seemed to be studying Sandy more and more carefully, until she ceased talking altogether, and continued to stare with a really strange look on her face.

"How's the baby?" She asked loudly, with a note of authority in her voice. Sandy looked stunned and I was shocked, for I couldn't remember telling her about the baby.

"*Where* is the baby?" She demanded, not waiting for a reply.

"Oh...the baby's adopted Mum..." I said casually. My stomach froze with the old familiar feeling of anxiety.

My mother continued to stare, and for a long moment appeared visibly upset. Then quite suddenly she dismissed the subject and - returning to the dining room - she briskly started to clear the table before moving out into the kitchen and beginning to wash up.

I was about to follow, but thought better of it, and closed the door quietly behind her, before whispering "Sorry about that."

The room was chilly, and Sandy sank into the small settee opposite the open fireplace, still dark with ash from the night before. She shivered and silently looked around the room, before saying,

"I feel really weird, as if something has walked over my grave".

"Yes. I did warn you she might act strangely at times."

"I don't think she was talking about my baby, and yet she was so adamant that it was."

"Well, I don't know what baby she was thinking about. I expect she has got you muddled with someone else. I don't remember telling her that you were pregnant, but I don't know…maybe I did".

"Should we go out and help her wash up?"

"No, it's best to leave her for a while. She will come in when she's ready."

Wishing to ease the atmosphere, I got up and took a photo of Dale, Keith and myself off the dark wooden mantle-piece. It was taken in our toddler days, and all looked remarkably clean in our well-ironed clothes. I passed it to Sandy.

"Look at our faces. We were obviously on our very best behaviour that day…"

Sandy laughed, remembering the stories I had told her about my brothers and I having wild play fights out of the upstairs window when my parents were out.

We took it in turns for one of us to fill a large tin mug from the bathroom tap, and randomly aim streams of water out the window at a shovel attached to a long pole taken from the coalbunker by the back door. The others ran around on the lawn, precariously waving this aloft in an attempt to stem the flow. A silly game, because we always missed and normally ended up drenched, but it was a lot of fun and certainly helped to ease the tension.

Sandy got up and started to look around the room. My mother loved pink and most times took care to ensure the room had heavy patterned drapes. As usual the walls were covered with the fashionable striped wallpaper of the day, although I cannot say it was really my taste. Dad wasn't a natural handyman, but dutifully took on the "man thing" of decorating every few years.

Sandy stopped for a moment, before taking down another photo off the television.

"Who is that?"

"My grandmother – my mother's mother."

Sandy looked closely at the picture of a wholesome young woman dressed in black, with her long dark hair parted in the middle and swept tight into a bun at the back. She looked a bit austere, but very elegant in the Victorian clothes of the time.

"Heavens!" Sandy exclaimed, "She looks like me!"

At that moment Mum appeared through the door, holding a jug of newly made lemonade. Putting it down on the side table she quickly took the photo, looked at it briefly and then stared hard at Sandy again.

"That's my mother - she died long ago." She carried on staring before abruptly turning away and adding, "Would you both like some lemonade and chocolate cake? I made them especially. Go and get the cake, it's in the kitchen."

"I'm really not hungry," whispered Sandy in the kitchen. "We've only just eaten."

"I know, but please have something, or she'll be upset."

When we returned to the lounge, my grandmother's photo was face down on the floor.

After that nothing much more was said, for the atmosphere had changed somehow. Sandy actually handled the situation very well, and tactfully altered the subject, admiring my mother's faux fur jacket that I had given her some while ago. Mum smiled and picked it up from the chair, looking quite pleased for moment,

"Do you really like it?" she asked, putting it on.

"Yes I do. It really suits you."

"Well, *you* have it then!"

She pulled it off roughly, and threw it across the room, bringing a rather abrupt ending to the harmony of the day.

And so, as discreetly as possible, we slowly made our departure.

****

When we returned home, I put Simon and Matthew to bed and Sandy went back to her place – for she wasn't living with me then. Luckily she didn't seem to be phased by the experience, and, after a rather intense discussion on our journey home - about the possible reasons for the sudden rather dramatic change of attitude – we decided to put it down to the unpredictability of my mother's illness.

Left with my thoughts, I still continued to peruse over what had happened, and the strange way Mum had looked at Sandy that day. Her remarks about the baby were odd too, but then that wasn't too unusual, for she had a way of suddenly going off at a tangent, apparently without a logical reason. However, I really felt certain that I had never mentioned the child to any of my family. We weren't in the habit of having long conversations on the phone and I couldn't imagine the information just slipping out.

Sandy's reaction to the photograph was extra-ordinary too. Her likeness to my grandmother was quite remarkable and probably why my mother had stared at her so hard. Mum was always telling me how psychic her mother was, so maybe she saw the same ability in Sandy? But that didn't explain the "baby" stuff, or why she had turned the picture face down.

I shook myself out of my reverie for I appreciated I must be an onlooker, and not a participant in this turn of events. Whatever the reality, something had touched a memory for both of them from long, long ago, and maybe the truth of it would appear in time.

I was just beginning to drift off to sleep when the door clicked open and Matthew padded in, rubbing his eyes in the brilliance of the moonlight that glistened through the window and across the room. My curtains were always left open at night.

"What's wrong?" I asked.

"There's a light at the end of my bed, and it keeps smiling at me."

He clambered up under the sheets. In a split second I conjured up a vision of a jolly little electric bulb, with spindly arms and legs, dancing around with a big grin on its face, and started to laugh. Matthew scowled.

"It's not funny! It keeps annoying me and I can't go to sleep."

"Are you frightened of it?"

"No." He contemplated for a minute. "It just sits

and watches me when I'm not looking."

"Oh dear. Well I'd better go and speak to it."

"Did you see it?" he asked when I returned.

"No." I thought I'd better tell him the truth.

"I didn't think you would. Simon can't see it either, but it *is* there!" He heaved a sigh.

"I know – I believe you." I remembered my own childhood and asked, "Can you see a snake at the end of this bed?"

He peered in front of him, suspiciously.

"No...."

"Well, there is one, but he's a special friend of mine, so you won't see him. Don't worry, - they are only friends who look after us – yours is probably a beautiful star."

"A Star?" he exclaimed.

"Yes, like those sparkly ones in the sky...see?" I pointed to them through the window. "Do you want to sleep in here tonight?"

"No thanks!" he retorted, with the aplomb of a 5 year old as he whisked out of the room, "I like my friend best!"

A few days later I overheard him wisely telling an old lady in the park, that he had a "Star with 5 legs" that sat on his bed at night, and "My Mummy goes to sleep with a snake." Where he got the '5 legs' from I had no idea, and I was glad I never saw the old lady again.

13 STUART'S ENTOURAGE

Due to the strange experience Sandy and I had encountered, it seemed that a doorway was opened, and a certain kind of closeness with my mother returned a number of times in varying forms over the following years.

We three shared another day alone together once, when Mum got out a number of old photographs of her family in younger days. She seemed inclined to open up much more when Sandy was around. There was only one further picture of my grandmother that I ever saw - dressed all in black, with a long coat, laced boots, and hair swept up under a large wide brimmed hat. I was intrigued that once again she did look remarkably like my friend. There were no photos of my grandfather, or any explanation as to why not, and I never saw those pictures again.

Another day Mum told me that she once had four little brothers and three died very young, before she was born – twins and another. Apparently that wasn't too unusual in those times, for medicine - particularly in India - was not very advanced. She also had a twin, who had died at birth, and I seriously wondered if that was why she kept mentioning "the baby", especially whenever Sandy appeared. However, when she talked, it was only at moments of her own choosing, and since she was always so quick to anger if questioned about the past, I was hesitant to keep asking.

Other times she divulged random stories about her days as a child. She particularly remembered when her mother played the old grand piano in the open hallway of their home in India. She was a wonderful pianist and at one time a member of the Royal Scottish National Orchestra. One day, being so involved in her music, she seemed completely unaware of a giant cobra swaying really close behind her, and didn't appear to notice when the snake was very loudly removed from the premises. However, she became greatly upset when discovering that it had been bludgeoned to death in the attack, for she said she was quite safe, and it would never have hurt her.

"Mother was very emotional, and very, very psychic" Mum once said, "She could always *see* what was going to happen, long before it did, but nobody believed her..." she paused, ruminating, before adding in a tone of resigned frustration, "They don't believe me, either...."

"How did Grandma die, Mum", I asked uncertainly, yet urgent to find some answers.

"She just died! She went out in the snow and died. She knew she was going to die, and told me.... " She stopped abruptly.

"But surely there isn't any snow in India?"

"It wasn't in India, it was in *Scotland!*" Her voice rose in irritation, "She begged me to stop them taking her away, but they wouldn't listen, and took her anyway. She told me she would die and I would never see her again.... And she was right wasn't she? - I *didn't!*".

I was absolutely horrified,

"Who were these people Mum, and why did she go out into the snow?"

"The Doctors! - They took her" She stared at me strangely. "... You know - you must remember that!" She added angrily, before lapsing into silence.

I certainly didn't know about the doctors, and realised she was probably muddled. I tried to get her to talk a bit more, but she blankly refused, and once again the moment was lost.

Each of these times brought me just a small step closer to finding out more about the deep anguish that haunted my mother, but the information was so slow in forthcoming, and other distracting events intervened along the way.   However, frustrating as it was at the time, I am absolutely sure now, that there is no such thing as co-incidence, but a series of teachings designed to lead us steadfastly to where our 'Inner Will' dictates - and when the time is right, all will become clear.

****

It was not long afterwards that I met David, who was soon to become my second husband. He, like me, had been married previously, and his two children, Chris and Debbie, were living with him.   We had a rather precarious courtship, which revolved around the youngsters more than ourselves, for our circumstances were very similar, and the children were only born a few weeks apart. It was like stalking around with two sets of twins and, instead of it being the battle of Simon and Matthew, it was now the battle of the four.

David was a policeman too, only totally unlike Paddy, for he was far more serious. We married in the spring, and - covered in confetti - met the children from school.   I suppose there is a lot I could say about my husbands, for they were good people at heart, but strangely their involvement was very small in comparison with the other events that have led to the writing of this book.   Because we lived so far from my parents they had little association with my mother - except on the rare visits - and seemed to rather indifferently accept the situation as it was, for most of the time.

David, like Adrian, wasn't the type of man to interest

himself in deep emotional speculation, and I felt obliged to hide a lot of the inner pain of my upbringing - including my continued determination to achieve my aim - from both my husbands, and indeed the rest of my family. Even the long discussions we used to have in my teenage years dwindled into insignificance, for my father seemed very tired at that time and needed to rest his mind on more mundane affairs, whilst my brothers were by now deeply involved in their own routines.

And so it was that, for the next seven years, life once again changed quite dramatically from deep concentration on more ethereal issues, to the earthly and mundane qualities of what one might call the "real" world.   But this time the contrast was not quite so defined, and the appearances of people and experiences followed one after the other in such perfect symmetry that it still astounds me today.

****

Stuart's entrance into my life was as dramatic as was his exit. David and I had opened a boutique in an arcade of shops in the Centre of Portsmouth, and Stuart was the landlord. One cold and blustering winter's day, he swept through the door of the shop, looking like a Toreador from Barbados, complete with wide brimmed hat and enormous billowing cape.

"I've a message from the front!" He announced looking furtively around.

"What front?" I asked, somewhat astounded.

"That front, at the back!" He bellowed, swiping an unfortunate customer in the face as he swung round with aplomb and pointed theatrically to the rear of the building.

There followed a series of fierce objections from the

woman whose jaw had nearly been broken, and profuse apologies, with sweeping gestures, from the lunatic who had suddenly entered my shop.

I looked on in stupefied amazement. Finally, he became aware of my presence again and, removing his hat, he bowed deeply.

"My name is Stuart," he remarked. "And I have a partner who isn't here because he's a complete dead-leg." Without another word, he swept down the aisle and disappeared from sight.

That was the man whom many have likened to the proverbial marmite - the most eccentric, bizarre and completely extraordinary person that anyone is ever likely to meet. Greatly admired or equally detested, he was someone with an electric quality that bound people to him with such force that only in the initial stages could they get away, and often those who stayed the course held scars of rejection and verbal onslaughts that were sometimes a long time healing.

Stuart came from the heart of the fashion world in London at the height of the sixties, where the business strategy seemed to require everyone to shout rather offensively at each other, whilst nobody bothered to listen or take offence. Not being the tallest of men, he had an uncanny resemblance to Napoleon Bonaparte - both in looks and performance. He was arrogant, loud, brash, blatantly truthful, and completely tactless - which he took great delight in admitting – yet his loyalty and unwavering commitment to the 'underdog' showed him to be a person of generous heart with firm principles, and for many years he became one of my closest and dearest friends.

There was something about him that reminded me of an intangible connection, long since forged but left dormant in the past. Many were the times an accidental glance would catch him with a look that was totally unlike him, yet somehow familiar, and I sincerely believe now that in the following years we worked through a situation that was a residue from another existence.

Shortly after my marriage to David, Stuart fell in love with Marilyn, a dark haired, vibrant and memorable young woman. She was one of those people with a Disney kind of face, rarely seen in real life - high cheekbones, large luminous eyes, and full lips that showed immaculate teeth when she smiled. She loved fine clothes, and wore them well, for she had an excellent figure and posture. She was indeed both a fascinating and very beautiful woman, and we got on brilliantly from the start.

It was not long before Marilyn, and her two little daughters, moved in with Stuart, and he happily took on the task of parenthood, for he had no children of his own. However, he was not the easiest person to live with, and given half a chance would completely dominate every situation, including Marilyn. Nevertheless, in many ways she was a perfect match for him, as she could cultivate the tongue of a fishwife when she chose, and had a strong tendency to tell the most whopping fibs in order to get her own way. Indeed, she would cheerfully admit on the quiet, that she had no compunction in using either of these, when fighting her corner.

Thus the four of us, became intrinsically involved in each other's lives, for they only lived across the road, and we spent many long hours together almost every day.

****

Once again I found myself returning to the everyday routine of marriage, children, and earning a living. David eventually left the police force to start his own career as an advanced driving instructor. From the beginning the fashion business was my domain, and over the next few years we aspired to the heights of owning four shops. I ran these without much difficulty, and the money came rolling in.

However, I didn't totally abandon my interests as in my previous marriage, for they had taken too great a hold by now, so I continued to question everything, and even tried to exchange theories with Stuart, who thought I talked a total load of nonsense anyway. He was another 'fact' merchant like my brother, and used to make jokes about me being 'super dramatic'. This was actually very true, but upsetting at the time.

"You know, I think there must be something wrong with me," I said to Marilyn once, after a dismal discussion about 'Man's inhumanity to Man' the previous day. As usual David and Marilyn had gone to sleep, and Stuart and I had ended up having the inevitable loud debate. "Perhaps I do get too intense, but it matters so much to me."

Marilyn glanced up from doing her make-up. She spent a lot of time on her appearance, although I never felt she needed to really. "There's nothing wrong with you," she said, in a rare profound statement, "You're just not with your kind of people. You belong with the hippies and the flower power community, where love is everything and money means nothing."

"But love *does* mean everything?"

She stopped and blotted her lips on a piece of tissue.

"Not to most people. It's difficult to love if you can't survive, and anyway, your sort of love is universal, not individual. Be glad if you're content with your dreams, for none of the rest of us are." She stood up, studying her face in the mirror, and smoothing her clothes, before adding,

"When you get old you are the sort of person who will always be happy. I won't, because old people lose their looks, and I don't want to be tired and grey. I will need a really good life style to make up for it."

I felt very sad, for I knew she had never really felt secure. She had been brought up in poverty, and, rejecting her schooling, I gather she became quite a wild teenager, who had two children and a failed marriage before she was twenty - which had obviously affected her greatly.

She told me once that she had really wanted to be a dancer, and had won a scholarship to a stage school. However, her father, who was a cautious and somewhat controlling man, thought it was a pipe dream and refused to let her go. She loved her father dearly, but I don't think she ever got over his denial, and resented very much being relegated to 'normal' motherhood, when she was not that way inclined and longed for a better life.

Still, Stuart was proud of her beauty and opened gateways for her to become a model   I remember watching her doing the "Dance of the Clowns" once, in a local fashion show. It was so unbelievably moving it made me cry, for I felt she was putting all the agony of her loss into this one beautiful and touching performance.

I watched her as she continued to brush her now blonde hair, which she was forever changing in colour and style. There was something about her own intensity that reminded me so much of my mother. I saw sadness, anger and bitterness there, and a great deal of underlying hurt, but it wasn't quite the same somehow. I couldn't catch within her the deep sorrow that was part of the real grief reflected in my mother's eyes. It seemed more like that of a disillusioned teenager who hadn't quite grown up, yet had been forced, far too early, to confront a life that she never really wanted.

Nevertheless, she had now become a beautiful woman, with plenty of money, and was certainly able to enjoy the good times. I really hoped this would continue for her, because by now we had become very close, and I cared about her very much.

However, as fortune turns, so life changes, and this time of apparent calm didn't remain with any of us for very long.

14 DOCTOR DEATH

Nobody noticed at first that I was spiralling down. Problems crept up in a silent, deceptive sort of way and in hindsight it became clear that deep emotional upsurges were warnings of ensuing trials.

Since the moment in my childhood, when seeing the trauma of my mother's illness, a pain had gripped me that can only be described as holding fast on my 'soul'. It wasn't always there, but seemed to be returning more and more. There appeared to be no apparent reason for it, as it was totally unconnected with anything tangible. I went for advice, but since the best way I could explain my condition was, 'Like my soul being torn apart', there was little doctors could do to help. It sounded so stupid when trying to describe it, that eventually I gave up, and resigned myself to having to live with it.

During my marriage I worked very hard, for it was no mean feat to run four shops in different parts of the country, and bring up four children that were moving fast towards their teens. For a while I seriously thought that 'rest' was all that was needed. However, the suppressed grief that I had been holding during the years of my youth was obviously attempting to draw attention to itself in an urgency to heal.

Everything, but everything seemed to hurt. It wasn't my own problems that affected me so much, for I can truthfully say that I didn't have any to speak of, but it was the media's insistence on accenting the horrors of the world that made me feel so terribly inadequate. I gave up watching The News, for it just wound me up to the point of anger at the pointlessness of it all. Stuart didn't agree though.

"You're losing touch with reality," he insisted. "You're always saying that suppression is bad, but what are you doing now if it isn't the same thing? Stop running away from life."

Being far too sensitive at the time, I couldn't take his advice on board, but many times later, whilst watching others going through the same kind of crisis, it became blatantly clear that all forms of suppression will take centre stage in time - if not through emotional release, then it will manifest as ill health. And that is exactly what happened to me.

Bit-by-bit, the illness appeared. I started to find that it was difficult to hold my balance; that often I was confronted with double vision. Many times I would drop things, for I was unable to hold them properly. Yet it wasn't a permanent condition. There were days of feeling fit and well, but other times of severe lack of co-ordination. My mind knew where it was going, but my body refused to react efficiently.

The difficulties grew more severe, and after consulting a specialist, I was told I was showing signs of Multiple Sclerosis. That was hard to believe, for I had grave doubts that I really had polio in my youth – the recovery, and ability to walk again, seemed far too rapid. Perhaps that was simply an emotional "blip", and maybe this was just another one? However, I was told it was very unlikely to be emotionally based.

Being determined to overcome this 'thing' that had invaded my life, I put all my energy into the believing that circumstances would soon improve. But the symptoms continued to get systematically worse, as if my body were grinding spasmodically to a halt. Finally, under pressure from people around, I was admitted to hospital for a lumbar puncture, to try to investigate the cause of the problem.

My theories on the ultimate power of the mind now seemed doomed to failure. This was an undeniable illness, and all the force of imagining I was going to get well, were of no avail. Had I been so wrong all these years about the answer to everything lying within one's control? Nevertheless, I resolutely refused to accept there was anything seriously amiss, and 'something' seemed to be telling me that I was putting myself at much greater risk by going through with the test at all.

It was in this traumatic state of mind that I entered the hospital.

I am still astounded by my subsequent complete lack of control, but it is important to explain how it happened, for the unremitting build up of emotion and resulting trauma involuntarily put me in a position where I made contact with a world that was not only beyond my own comprehension, but certainly that of many people today.

In the 1970s the medical approach was extremely different from the way it is now, and – almost certainly because of my mother - I rarely trusted doctors to be open with the truth, and indeed felt very suspicious of their propensity to find solutions with pills.

It was with considerable fortitude that the medical profession put up with it all, for I was probably one of the worst patients they could possibly come across; having no faith in their diagnosis or judgments, yet still proceeding to thunder into their territory and demand to be helped. It shames me now that I felt like this, for without their exceptional dedication, astounding insight and ability, many a seriously ill patient, including myself, would have surely died.

The day I entered hospital, they took my clothes away – or I felt certain of the fact. I thought they had hidden them, and had an erratic argument with a student nurse who tried to stop me when I went off in search of them.

Getting no joy, I stalked up to a stern looking Sister

who was peering suspiciously as she bustled down the Ward.

"My clothes are not in my locker" I thought I sounded polite, but her response was brusque.

"Well, I'm sure we'll find them later"

"Hmm...but I want to know where they are now!"

"I have things to do at the moment. It's nothing to worry about. You won't need them today."

With that, she turned on her heels and started to wander back up the Ward. This was not the result I wanted, so I began to pad along directly behind her, with hushed determined strides. When we reached the end of the ward, she swung round and stared at me uncomfortably.

"Why don't you go back to bed, and I will be there in a minute?"

"Ok", I said, as casually as I didn't feel. I didn't get into bed though, but stood beside it waiting whilst she spoke at length to some man in a white coat, whom I presumed was a doctor. I stared at them with immense intensity, and knew they were very aware of my concentration. Eventually she disappeared for a moment and returned, walking back up the ward with a patient smile on her face.

"Is that my doctor you were talking to?", I queried.

"Yes – Dr Deth. He's a very good doctor."

"Dr Death?" I stared at her dumbfounded.

"Yes, Dr Deth. He will be seeing you tomorrow."

"Dr Death!" I repeated feeling decidedly alarmed. She nodded, quite un-fazed, and seemingly amused by

my concern.

"Well ... " I cleared my throat anxiously. "I would like to speak to him, please"

"He is very busy right now."

"Too busy to talk to a patient? I thought that was his job!" My voice rose in frustration.

She gave me an exasperated glance. "Now then, there's no need to get excited! Everything is all right! Why don't you get into bed and take this...." She drew out a tiny white pill from her pocket. I stared at it incredulously. What did I want a pill for? I only wanted to see a doctor.

"Why are you giving me pills?"

"It will make you feel better." She held it towards me.

I sat down heavily on the end of a bed. The conversation was obviously going nowhere. I tried to compose myself and soften my voice.

"All I want to do is see this doctor and find out exactly what they're going to do tomorrow." I said as slowly and as quietly as possible.

"There's time enough to see the doctor then. Now, why don't you be sensible? You'll feel much better if you get into bed, and take this...." ...and there was the pill again!

"Look!" I hissed. I was trying to sound friendly, but it came out like a snarling snake. "I don't *want* your pill. *You* can have it if you like. I just want to have a quiet conversation with someone who'll explain *what the hell they are going to do to me tomorrow!*"

"My dear!" she was obviously trying to keep her

temper, "You're getting far too excited. What *is* worrying you?"

I tried to explain to her very loudly that it was only her that was worrying me, with her pills and patronising voice, but she wasn't about to believe me, so I gave up abruptly, and decided that, if she wouldn't talk any sense I would find someone who would. By now, however, she didn't trust me at all, and kept a stringent watch from her vantage point at the end of the ward.

Looking for an escape, I sat trying to decide what to do. The more time went on, the more I became certain that there was no alternative but to leave the hospital before something really bad happened. The instinct was so deeply intense and apparently of vital importance – just as if I was being directed by someone outside myself.

When the night shift came on, I eventually saw my chance, and shot off, in a mad Pink Panther type sprint, up the corridors in a hectic search for any other doctor I could lay my hands on. But it was a waste of time, because I was obviously behaving like a wild thing by then, and people with tight faces kept handing me back to the Ward. Rapidly exhaustion took over and, becoming too upset to argue, I found myself in a room on my own, with a pacing matron on guard outside.

I leant hard against the door, and started to cry silently. All this had come out of a simple question, and the more they wouldn't answer, the worse it had got. Everything was telling me that the test I was about to have was far more dangerous than the illness. Coupled with that - in my frame of mind - discovering that the name of my consultant was Dr Death, completely put the Ki-bosh on everything.

Walking over to the basin, I splashed some cold water on my face before peering in the mirror whilst drying it with a towel. I looked a frightful sight, draped in one of those ghastly white backless gowns, with tapes hanging everywhere, and my hair stood on end.

In spite of my trauma, I was suddenly amused. Goodness, those poor people must have thought I was a complete nutcase. I made a contorted face at myself in the mirror and started to grin rather inanely, when the most astonishing thing happened. A huge male voice, from somewhere behind me, bellowed,

"Go from this place! Take up your sword and fight!"

I swung round in shock, but there was absolutely nobody in the room. Hurriedly I opened the door, but there was only the matron glowering at me from a distance outside, so I closed it again rapidly and sat down on the bed.

"Now then," I said out loud, feeling completely stunned, "either, my dear, you have gone totally mad, or you really heard that! Which is it?"

I seriously didn't know. To me the Voice was as real as reality could be. It was very loud, very clear, and very male - but then people who were supposed to be mentally ill often heard loud, clear voices. I could understand how people could think I was mad, from the way I had behaved that day, but I could also see how people could be driven nearly mad by the way I was handled that day.

Sympathy for my mother welled up. I knew what it was like to be on the other side of it now – trying to talk to people who wouldn't listen - people who made judgments on the way you felt; insisted you conform to their silly rules, and gave you pills to shut you up.

No, after some consideration, I really didn't think I was mad. Seriously lacking control certainly, but not mad. Yes, I *had* heard a voice all right and I couldn't dispute it - though or course, others would. But whatever it was, fact or fantasy, it had helped me to decide what was right for me. Ultimately, in spite of the opinions of others, I was the one who would have to live with it.

The following morning a sprauncy battle-axe of a nurse woke me at the crack of dawn - talking in a bright sunny voice about sunny bright things, and puffing up the pillows in a flurry of activity. Later, after a dismal breakfast, in trooped the famous "Dr Death", and a couple of people I had attacked the previous day. They stood by the bed, and peered down, as if I was some microscopic specimen of dubious origin.

"I hear there has been a small problem," the doctor said, as an understatement.

Still feeling a bit irritable, I quite tactlessly explained that the only problem lay in my desire to know the risks involved in the test, and the stupid mania they seemed to have for shoving pills down everyone's throats. I dared him to tell me the truth and, with much reluctance, he explained.

****

"Well, that's all right then." I thought to myself as I left the hospital. "Just a slight risk of being paralysed for the rest of your life, that's all!"

On my way home, I realised that, if I hadn't shown such obvious signs of trauma, I may well have got a straight answer to my questions. But then, if I had been told the simple truth in the first place, it was unlikely that the ensuing dramatic events would have occurred.

Yes, indeed I had behaved extremely stupidly, but I really *had* heard an immensely loud voice instructing me to leave. The whole thing had been an extraordinary experience, but crazy or not, my intuition was telling me very loudly that something would seriously go amiss if I stayed in that place.   As a patient, I was expected to conform to the normal routine of hospital life, but I didn't fit into the natural categories, and I suppose that's were it all went wrong.

"If you had no intention of going through with the tests, you shouldn't have gone in the first place and wasted everyone's time." Stuart announced when he saw me.

"But I did have good intentions," I argued.   "All I wanted was the truth..." He cut across me.

"Right! But you were only searching for the truth in yourself not the situation!   That's actually lying, and it's a terrible thing to make everyone worry, whilst you're struggling with your own beliefs."

I was really upset when he said that, for I thought I was telling the truth, but I didn't understand then, that the mind has a way of lying to itself in such a way as to even confuse the innermost thoughts of the person who speaks them.

"People see only what they want to see" my grandmother had once said, and I don't even know whether she or anyone else knew how important their statements would become to me, when I had made sufficient growth to understand their meaning.

15 DOCTOR SINGHA

During the previous months, I had remained only very briefly in touch with my family, and chose not to mention my illness, as I really couldn't deal with my mother's involvement, or the thought of putting extra pressure on my father.

By then Keith had left home and married, and we all lived some distance from each other. I hardly ever spoke at all with either of my brothers, and we seemed to fall into the routine of never phoning and only meeting on very rare occasions. We were each so different, and didn't have much in common really. So, for quite a long while, there was little association.

Due to the strangeness of our childhood, I think we were more drawn together by the unpredictability of events than strong familiarity. Dad was from the "Old School", which was quite normal then – men did cars, and pubs, and "men's" things, and women did knitting, and other sparkling things like cooking and stuff. Unfortunately I didn't fit into the right category, and was far more interested in joining in "their" kind of world, which made me feel frustrated and angry at times – especially when Dad wouldn't let me learn to drive when I was young, because Mum would insist on learning as well.

I suppose my brothers and I hadn't really got to know each other that well, and, as we grew older I felt that neither of them wanted to discuss how they felt about previous events – the subject was obviously quite emotionally charged. We weren't encouraged to talk about our personal feelings really as we grew up – because of Mum's illness I suppose, but it was also a sign of the times. People generally tried to deal with things in their own way, which probably did a lot to build unhealthy skeletons in family closets.

Maybe that was why I put so much intellectual accent on everything as I searched for solutions, and, as talking about our past had become something of a forbidden area, it was easier to continue looking for answers alone.

****

Two weeks following my return from hospital, someone mentioned an acupuncturist in London. He was highly recommended and apparently his methods showed great results. Still needing to solve my dilemma, I found the idea fascinating. This consultant turned out to be one of the most profound and adept of practitioners that I have ever been lucky enough to meet.

Of course, there have been great advances in public understanding of alternative treatments since the time I first took this action. However, although acupuncture is generally accepted these days, the holistic approach is still not always appreciated, and there were a number of things explained to me at the time that probably continue to remain in their infancy in the medical world today.

Dr Singha was Indian, which surprised me at first, for I thought the Chinese had the monopoly in the field of acupuncture. He examined me carefully and, after a while, made no bones about my condition.

"You have," he said in his Indian accent, "what we would call the illness of the nervous system. In the Western World there is no cure but, contrary to Western belief, we are able to do something about it. It is a question of diet, and belief in that diet. And it is a question of the mind and belief in yourself."

This statement was a complete revelation to me 40 years ago, and I became totally captivated by his beliefs.

Nevertheless, he initially seemed to have the most extraordinary ideas, insisting that I should stop eating anything that was cooked for the next two weeks. In case you don't know, this is decidedly hard.

At first, I thought of lovely things like munching doughnuts, toast and marmalade with lots of butter, and cereal - in fact many extravagances I loved. But of course all these things are actually processed in one way or another, so, to my disgust, I was left to plough through grapefruit and grapes for what seemed like an eternity. He told me to boil an onion and drink the water once! Yet strangely, putting aside my usual perversity, I always did as he asked – and along with his needles, felt considerably better for it.

Over the next few months, I learned a great deal about diet and the effect it can have on the physical wellbeing as well as the mental attitude of the patient. I began, very slowly to recover, but it was a long haul, with some setbacks along the way, for my condition had been pretty poor when I arrived at his surgery.

"What exactly is the diet supposed to do?" I asked one day. He never seemed to mind my numerous questions.

"It clears the body of toxic wastes." he replied. "You Western people fill yourselves with all sorts of poisons and we have to clear them away. There are so many foods that are poison to some people but not to other people. You have had an allergy to gluten. It makes you ill outside in the body. Some people have allergies to things that make them ill inside in the mind," he pointed to his forehead.

"How's that?" I queried.

"Reaction to the food puts a substance into the brain which is not very good."

"A chemical?" I asked, thinking of my brother's comments in the past.

"I don't know a chemical," he said indifferently. "It is a substance that comes from an allergy to the food they eat."

"And if they find out what the allergy is they'll stop being ill?"

"Well.... do you feel better?"

"Yes indeed," I said adamantly

"Well" he repeated. "If the body can get better, then so can the mind"

So a chemical reaction in the brain didn't have to be treated by drugs. It could be treated by food - the natural way. I wondered why on earth the medical profession didn't seem interested in the idea.

"So all mental illness is caused by an allergy to food?"

"Oh no!" he laughed. "It is also to do with their emotions and their attitude of mind towards their worries - some people worry, worry, worry all the time. When we are frightened we release adrenalin into the system. When we are emotionally disturbed we release other things that can have an affect on the mind". He looked at me severely before adding,

"In India we are taught to look after more than the physical body. We also look after the emotional, mental and spiritual bodies. These four bodies go to make up the whole person. Each one reacts to the others like a continuous line. We need to look after them all. Western people do not understand this."

I was silent for a moment taking in what he had said. It was a revelation to me and so many bits of the puzzle seemed to be slotting into place.

"Can you cure everything then?" I ventured. He smiled and shook his head.

"You must understand that I don't pretend to cure anything," he said, "The human being is a magnificent example of the perfect balance of nature. It should be at ease with itself. When it is out of balance it brings lack of ease, or 'dis-ease' as people say. All I do is put things back in balance and the disease goes away. I do not cure you. You do it yourself."

"I am feeling so much better" I ruminated quietly

"Good. Good." he replied casually. "Well, I'm not your Jesus Christ, but I am trying very hard!"

I travelled home, my head pounding with newfound understanding. In one short conversation this wise and patient man had confirmed so many of the opinions of others that appeared to be contradictory - my brother's belief in the chemical reaction in the brain, my father's belief in the correct attitude of mind, and the spiritualist's belief in the four bodies of man. Far from any one of them having to be wrong, they were all perfectly right.

The job of a doctor, nutritionist, or alternative practitioner, was obviously to endeavour to restore balance. If the natural process of nature was disturbed, then the chain reaction could bring about a breakdown of health in *any* of the spiritual, mental, emotional or physical bodies. These people were really the 'mechanics' that attempted to intervene in the continuous spiral of life, and tried to re-adjust any problems, just as the garage mechanic balanced the wheels of a car.

For me, it was vitally important to try to find some positive proof that the mind was indeed able to seriously affect the health.

Little did I know how soon I would get that personal proof, for the events that were soon to follow were to become a dramatic moment of confrontation to my seemingly unshakable faith.

****

It was sometime in the autumn of the same year that I first spoke to my friend Angie about her own problems. Things had been difficult for her for some while, and she had sought advice from the doctor, but he hadn't seriously considered there was anything wrong.

"It's not that I feel terribly ill," she confided one day, as we sat together over teacakes in the coffee bar that I now owned. "It's just that I know inside there is something wrong; something very wrong, yet they tell me it's psychological. Do you think that's possible?"

I laughed, "Oh yes, very possible! My particular case is a typical example. I'm convinced that the mind can do very strange things."

"Well, if that's true, why can't we control it?" she asked.

"I don't know. I've wondered that myself. As a child I had polio, but when I think about it, the symptoms are not unlike the sort of symptoms I'm showing now. Perhaps they are linked together in some way."

Angie looked at me seriously, "I think you're a fool," she said. "You never allowed them to do the tests to find out, but you don't seem to bother or care."

"Yes, I suppose it does seem stupid," I agreed, "but I just believe that what I am doing is right for me. In your case, if you really believe there is something wrong, in spite of what you've been told, it may be wise to get a second opinion. It's what *you* feel that counts, not what other people say."

"Yes, I suppose you're right. Perhaps I'll do that." She gazed into her coffee, seemingly lost in thought.

I looked at her closely; she didn't appear on the surface to be ill at all. She was so very pretty, petite and blonde, with a wonderful smile and a lovely sense of humour. Everyone was very fond of Angie. I had known her for years, from way back in the days when I was between marriages and used to sit and drink thousands of coffees in her dress shop in Gosport. I had met both Paddy and David through her. I can't say we were ever very close friends, but our paths seemed to be continually crossing.

What used to be a group of small shops - known as The Village - had now been rebuilt after a terrible fire. Inside it was magnificent in size and splendour, for Stuart saw to it that it looked one of the most impressive places in town. Within the area, as before, were a number of privately owned shops, rather like a small arcade. Angie owned one of these on the ground floor.

By now, I was in the process of selling our other shops, and at 35 years had tried, rather stupidly as it turned out, to launch myself into the catering business. It was ridiculous really, for I was probably the worst cook in living memory, and I'm sure the coffee became famous for being impossible to drink. Still, we were making a living. I used to regiment the kids into action, and we had a lot of fun whilst preparing mountains of food every day.

"What are you doing?" Stuart's voice bellowed suddenly from behind, making us jump in shock.

"Nothing!" we replied in unison.

"That's just it, you never do anything!" He picked up our cups from the table and piled them precariously on his arm, before transporting them from there to the till. He turned round as we watched him.

"Everyone is so terribly boring. They are always doing nothing," and, with a gesture of disgust, followed by a wide grin, he vanished into the hairdressers alongside us.

"I'm Stuart" we heard him say to a bewildered customer in enormous rollers. "Good afternoon!"

16 ANGIE'S PROMISE

It was shortly after that when Angie took a second opinion, and was immediately advised that she had cancer. An operation was performed, and within two weeks she was back, looking as lively as ever - but the joy at her recovery was not to be.

Less than a month later, her condition deteriorated severely and, with mounting shock, we heard that she had been given a very short time to live. I was absolutely appalled for it seemed to me that the operation had only accelerated her illness. Previously she had felt ill, but not dramatically so, yet now, within weeks, there was nothing of her short life she was able to enjoy.

"I haven't even been given the chance to go out and get run over by a bus," she said when I went to see her. She had lost two stone in weight by then and, in spite of her attempted bravery the tears welled up in her eyes and rolled silently down her cheeks. I looked back at her with a tightness in my throat that made it increasingly difficult to reply.

"I keep thinking of the conversation we had in your coffee bar," she went on, fidgeting continuously with the edge of the blanket that was wrapped around her fragile body. "You were so convinced that your illness was an illusion that you fought against all the doctors' advice. I wish to God I had believed in what I knew inside, and had the courage of my convictions to challenge them too. Maybe if I had done so, my disease would have been discovered long before it was too late."

I tried to answer her, fighting back my own tears. "It's nobody's fault," I managed to say finally. "We just need to recognise that everyone can make mistakes, even those in authority. We tend to forget that they too are also human. But who knows, I could be wrong about myself even now."

She shook her head slowly, "No, I don't think you are, but even if it turns out to be true, you would know that it was your own mistake and nobody else's. That's what you were trying to tell me weren't you? To believe in yourself and your own judgements until you've proved to yourself you are wrong?"

I was silent, not knowing quite how to reply, but she didn't seem to notice.

"You're not frightened of dying are you?" she asked.

"No."

"Why not?"

"Maybe because I know there is more to life than just living here on earth. It continues afterwards in other worlds."

"I wish I could believe that. I don't want to die. I so badly want to live. It seems totally unfair that I have to face this now, when I'm only just thirty and there's such a lot to do. I'm so terribly frightened. If only I had your faith. I wish you could give me some of your faith...." She was crying openly now; heart breaking sobs of futility, anger and fear, and I felt desperately inadequate, for there was nothing I could do to ease her pain.

I put my arms around her, rocking her gently and searching for words that would mean something. Something she could touch; that would be real to her, and not just abstract words of 'faith' in an elusive Creator.

"It's the not knowing *why* that hurts so much," she

whispered finally. "If I only knew why, I might be able to accept it..."

All at once I remembered the conversation with my father and the picture that he had taken from the wall. Perhaps there was some way I could help her after all. Carefully I went through the sequence as my father had done with me, and slowly, bit-by-bit her tears started to subside.

"I think I understand a little more now," she said eventually. "Maybe if I sleep awhile, things will become clearer to me. I'm so very tired." I left the room quietly, but she was already breathing peacefully.

Yet, in spite of the fact I was perhaps able to ease a little of the burden that had been thrust upon her, I found myself very angry inside. There were reasons, I knew there were reasons, and I completely accepted that the picture of life was so large we could never comprehend it completely. But that didn't excuse the errors and incompetence displayed not only by others, but ourselves within a situation.

How the hell were we supposed to know or learn anything if we weren't educated to understand ourselves; to recognise the symptoms in our own bodies instead of relying on the judgements of others who couldn't really be blamed for making mistakes sometimes?

We were not allowed to take responsibility for ourselves - not in our religion, not in our health and not even in our everyday life. There was always someone who was convinced by the authority of a textbook qualification that they knew better than us.

For a while after that, Angie's attitude seemed to improve. She never spoke again of the reasons why things were happening. She seemed to have gained some sort of acceptance, but still hung on with grim commitment to the remains of her life. Her bravery was astounding and, even amongst her terrible suffering, she retained a wonderful composure - yet I knew that underneath, the anger and resentment of her condition was driving her to snatch with desperate determination the last straws of her life.

"They told me I wouldn't live to Christmas," she said the last time I saw her. "But I proved them wrong, didn't I?" She looked at me with wide hollow eyes that still held a note of her past beauty. "If I imagine I'm well hard enough, I may get better. It's all in the mind isn't it? You said it was."

"Yes," I answered, but I knew, with grim finality, that it wasn't going to work for her. If anyone wanted to live, and had a chance to prove that 'belief' would heal, it was Angie. Yet nothing was happening - just a slow, insidious slipping over the edge like someone clutching frantically onto the side of a cliff.

Why didn't it work? What was wrong with everything? And why couldn't I do it for myself either?

A terrible emptiness was building up inside that I tried to avoid her seeing. My faith was slipping systematically away along with the last remnants of her life. It was all so pointless - the struggle, the hope. Where did it all lead us? We might as well give up for we'd never win. As I fought to quell the mounting fury and frustration inside me, she spoke - as if she knew how I felt.

"I won't see you again," she said simply. "Go now. Everyone has done all they can. If there is truth in what you say - that life continues - then I will let you know somehow. Believe in that for me. I will let you know! It's a pact between us. Go now. I must sleep."

I kissed her gently before leaving the room and, once alone, I cried as I had never done since the night of my mother's illness, so many years before.

Two days later, we heard that Angie had died, but I already knew. That same night, as I lay tossing and turning in my sleep, I heard footsteps passing beside me, and the light was switched on at the table. I looked for David, but he was fast asleep, and I knew that Angie was gone.

I still couldn't quell the anger at the way of her death, for it seemed to me that she was doomed from the beginning to a series of errors and confusion in her treatment that had ganged up against her as a terrible hand of fate. She was meant to die, there was no doubt, and it was only in my solid belief in the perfect justice of Karma that I could find any solace.

The following day I went into the Village as usual, to try and keep my mind occupied and away from the continuous round of questions that had invaded my thoughts, but it was to no avail. I was filled with a burning intensity to find an answer - any answer - not just to the question of mental health, but to all health - my illness, Angie's illness; Any illness!

If God was the architect and the doctors the mechanics, what was the oil that lubricated the machine and helped it run smoothly and free from fault? It wasn't drugs, it wasn't pills and it wasn't operations. Was it *really* the mind? And if it was, why in God's name didn't it work when you believed and tried so very hard to use it?

I busied myself with the cabinet in the coffee bar. It was ladled with cakes and food ready for the incoming crowd. The place was half full already, and a queue waited expectantly for staff to serve them. I stared fiercely at a gateau in front of me, still concentrating on my thoughts, and to my amazement, the glass shelf it was placed upon, split across with a resounding crack and tumbled into the display cabinet, making all of us jump in shock.

"How very odd!" I commented to the astounded faces in front of me as I picked up the pieces and looked at them carefully. "The glass is so thick and solid, I just can't see how it could have broken in so many pieces - and leave the gateau still in tact."

Just at that moment, we all became aware of a loud commotion going on downstairs. People seemed to be shouting and making a big issue about something. Somewhat alarmed, a number of individuals hurriedly followed me downstairs and into Angie's shop. It was full of staff and a horrified looking customer.

"I was just looking in the mirror, when it cracked from top to bottom," she spluttered, reiterating the story for the umpteenth time. "I've heard of *faces* breaking glass, but I've never seen it happen! I can't believe it...*I can't believe it!*" she repeated, laughing rather shakily, "What a silly thing to happen!"

Now of course people will say that I immediately thought that this event was Angie making contact as she had promised – and of course I did! How could it really be classified as merely a coincidence? It was too much of a coincidence. The glass in my place and Angie's had smashed at the same time. There were many witnesses to prove it, and nobody could logically explain it away.

Stuart couldn't explain it either, but then he wasn't there at the time. Besides, if Stuart couldn't explain things, then - as far as he was concerned – it was obviously just a 'trick' of an over vivid imagination.

So, it seemed more sensible not to openly disclose the secret pact Angie and I had made between us, although a few people already knew. If I *was* just imagining this was a communication she was sending me, then at least I'd found the incentive to believe again in the power of the mind. It just needed effort and time to understand, that's all. Just effort and time...

****

It wasn't until a few weeks later that I realised for certain I was no longer ill. All my faculties had returned to me completely. At first I thought it was one of my usual passing phases of health, but I felt different inside somehow, and I knew in my heart that it wasn't just make believe. Something had surely happened. An experience so powerful and healing that it was no longer necessary for my continued visits to the acupuncturist.

Yes, something *had* happened to my mind - an intangible and inexplicable event, but it gave me some proof. Proof perhaps that few would accept, but it was certainly enough for me. Somewhere in the mind was the power that controlled these things, and I knew I would find it one day.

Many years have passed since that time in 1976, and people are far more open in their beliefs – yet for those who were not privy to such events, there must always be some element of doubt, however small?

Nevertheless, it is not for me to try and convince anyone of the truth, but to point out for your own observation the circumstances that later followed, which led me to realise just how powerful the mind can be in bringing about the most extraordinary of things.

17 TRUTH AND THE THREE WISE MEN

I suppose it would be fair to say that my marriage never really recovered from the onslaught of that year. I don't think either David or I were aware of it at the time, but on-going problems were becoming larger and more difficult to handle.

Our relationship with Stuart and Marilyn intensified, and hardly a day went by that we didn't spend in each other's company, which I suppose in many respects was a necessary diversion. We might have all muddled on in that way together for many more years, but fate took a hand in our lives, and John walked in through the door. Poor John. He had nothing to do with the rift between David and I, but for a long time afterwards he was blamed for the break up of our marriage.

I guess everything might have been all right if Marilyn hadn't fallen for him immediately. But then, that was very easy to do, for John was a big golden cockney from the heart of London - a shining sun of laughter and fun, who held a magical quality that seemed to draw everything to him with confidence and ease. And this, of course, didn't go down at all well in Stuart's world.

Marilyn and John had a brief fling, and at first sight, the events that ensued, seemed very like that of a situation comedy. However as time rolled on, it became very clear to me that we were all caught up in a dreadful karmic whiplash that was certain to have a radical affect on all our lives.

The story was very theatrical; never ending, and to explain in detail would be of little value – except for the very important point that it sadly brought the end of my marriage and threw me headfirst into some of the oddest but most valuable discoveries of my life. It is enough to say that David, Marilyn, Stuart and myself were ripped apart in the onslaught, and we all learned very hard lessons on the real meaning of truth in the process - truth about ourselves that is.

The problem I faced amongst it all was one of loyalty - loyalty to two extremely volatile people in a deeply hostile and broken relationship - and I learned the bitter truth that it was not acceptable to remain loyal to both, because apparently life simply doesn't work that way.

Many people take sides at times like this, but I found it virtually impossible. Coupled with that I foolishly allowed Stuart and Marilyn, to use me as both their confidant and mediator. The ultimate cost, of course, was to discover that this was very stupid, for we were far too entangled in a ridiculous situation.

Due to circumstance, it also became very obvious that David and I were growing further and further apart, for we rather dramatically discovered that there were things we both needed within a relationship that neither could give. It was a hard realisation and our marriage couldn't withstand the strain, as I suppose it was too fragile before we started.

The wedding of Stuart and Marilyn was probably the last time the four of us socialised together, and I am ashamed to say that I cried right through it – for, after the ferocity of recent times, it seemed to me the most dreadful of mistakes. It was a very sudden arrangement, right in the midst of the fiasco, and likely brought about more from dented pride than anything else. This turned out to be a sad portent for the future, as it was inevitable that they would later divorce.

It was not long after the marriage that Stuart gave an ultimatum, which required me to make a direct choice between continuing the friendship with himself - or not if I continued to see anything of John. I suppose this was understandable for he obviously wanted to avoid any chance of Marilyn seeing John again, but it was extremely difficult to comply with his demands, for it sounded very much like emotional blackmail to me. Stuart was definitely a far more important friend at that time, but, despite our closeness, I felt unable to accept such direct coercion, and it was on one sunny summer's evening that I watched in desolation as he walked out the door and out of my life.

In the 5 years that followed I saw nothing of Stuart and very little of Marilyn.   David and I remained distant friends, and still are today.   I was his second wife, and to date he has now married 6 in all – that by itself tells another story, and I actually got to know three of them quite well!   Chris and Debbie joined him shortly after we parted, and there we were, back in very much the same situation as before, only seven years later.

I knew then that I had to make some radical decisions on the direction I had been taking, for there were so many unanswered questions as to why it had happened, and could it happen again?

"You tried to play God." Stuart had said to me, not long before we parted. "You shouldn't have done that for you were bound to fail. We all believed in you and you failed!"

It was a very harsh statement and I said so, for it wasn't my fault how things had occurred, but he wouldn't be diverted.

"You're always harping on about the truth, but you don't even speak it yourself - you tried to play God, and you weren't God."

"That's terribly unfair," I announced in frustration and near to tears. "One thing I don't do is lie!"

"Not even to yourself?" retorted Stuart. "That's the

worst lie of all!" He was pacing the floor as he spoke.

"What on earth do you mean?" I exploded.

Stuart gave an irritated shrug; "You live in another world, full of principles and prophesies, but no reality when it comes down to it."

"How can you say that?" I was furious and very hurt. "My beliefs are certainly not an illusion!"

"Aren't they?" he glowered. "Beliefs are all pie in the sky until they're brought down to earth and used for a purpose."

"Well, what do you think I've been doing all through this saga? Another person would have taken sides and been done with it!"

"Trying is not enough! You *should* have taken sides. This is real life. I was your closest friend – closer than Marilyn, and definitely closer than John. It would have been more honest to take sides"

I was silent for a minute trying to grasp his meaning,

"Well, I really don't know what's so wrong in being able to see all sides of things. You all involved me - I didn't involve myself!"

"Maybe not in your eyes perhaps, but you were there!"

"I could hardly be anywhere else! We see each other nearly every day."

"You could have said NO!"

"No to what, and to whom? - Refusing to listen when you all insisted on talking to me about it? That's hardly being a good friend to anyone."

"You couldn't solve it, anyway". He glanced out of the window with a resigned sigh. "How could you if you don't really know yourself, and are not aware of your own limitations?"

"I think I know myself very well...."

"Right!" He cut me short, "I'm sure you think you do, but you don't. Nobody knows who they are really. That's half the problem."

That conversation continuously came back to me in the weeks that followed, and one evening I just couldn't let the subject go. What did he mean? What did I do that was so wrong? If anyone was in constant surveillance of character, it was myself. I was the original seeker of truth. I knew my failings, and didn't mind admitting them, so where on earth was it all at?

I went to the fridge to pour a glass of wine. Perhaps I really did live in another world after all? With glass in hand, I sat down at the kitchen table, and picked up a new book on Astrology. I flipped open the cover, and there before me I noticed the following quote,

"Whatever is born or done this moment of time, has the qualities of this moment of time" Carl Jung.

I looked hard at the name - *Carl Jung*. He was a well-recognised psychologist. Whatever was his name doing after a quote in this book? This jogged my memory, for although I always knew he was interested in Astrology, I had clearly overlooked the significance in my teenage days

Astrologers seriously believed that there were psychological benefits to be found in the correct interpretation of the subject, but I never seemed to have been able to come to grips with the process of setting up a chart properly.

Of course! If Carl Jung believed in Astrology, and used it in his work, then surely it had to hold a vital key of importance for someone like my mother? He was a well-respected and eminent psychologist, who was not only quoted in the book, but had actually studied it himself - a subject long since ridiculed and dismissed by scientists in the west, yet confusingly, encompassed by others in the east.

Somebody said to me once, "You will always know when you're ready to understand, for the information or teacher you need will appear in front of you." How true this statement was, for from the moment I started to look at the subject from a different angle, things seemed to tumble into my lap.

The very next day, without any effort on my part, a leaflet was pushed through the door. It was from the Education Authority and there amongst the Needlework and Astronomy, were details of classes on Astrology.

Well, of course I leapt in from a great height and, dragging poor Sandy with me, we descended, feet first, into the introductory lesson.

I don't think the lecturer knew what hit him. His name was Rupert, and in many ways he was remarkably like the bear, only he wore glasses and was incredibly intelligent. I remember thinking that if I had half his brains, I would be brilliant, and for the first hour of the lesson I felt as if we had walked into a higher-level tutorial in Nuclear Physics.

Sandy was horrified, and kept whispering in a loud monotone - mainly because she's a bit deaf,

"What's he saying?"

I was finding it hard enough to listen myself, so I kept hissing back intermittently,

"Shut up! I'll tell you later..." until at last I began to get some grasp of what he was saying.

It became abundantly clear that Rupert himself was extremely interested in the psychological aspects of Astrology. However, a great deal of what he said seemed to be going straight over my head, and what with all the muttering going on between Sandy and myself, I began to lose concentration.

But suddenly, in the midst of all the fidgeting and scuffling, my attention was caught by a name, which seemed to resound out across the room.

"Excuse me!" I said rather rudely cutting across him in mid-sentence, "Sorry, but what did you just say?"

"I was talking about the scientist Newton, who said, when he was challenged about Astrology, *'Sir, I have studied it, and you have not!'*"

"*Newton?*" I repeated.

"Yes."

"*Isaac Newton?* You mean he was an Astrologer?"

"Yes!" he laughed. "That's not so strange. Quite a few scientists were Astrologers. Take Einstein for instance...."

"*Einstein?* Good heavens!" I was stunned. "I thought scientists ridiculed Astrology."

"Well there you are. Not all of them did, but, as I've said, they came under fire from other scientists because of it."

I was silent through the rest of the lesson, determined now to get to grips with the subject once and for all. If it was good enough for Einstein, Newton and Jung, then there *must* be something in it that was worth looking into more deeply.

From then on I think poor Rupert rued the day that we ever met, for I couldn't contain myself from asking a million questions.

One thing puzzled me, however. There didn't seem to be conclusive answers as to why Astrology worked. Most people just accepted that it did work, but would that have been enough for the three scientists? I was absolutely certain in my own mind that logical interpretation of a horoscope must have a great deal to do with it.

By now Simon had grown into a strapping fifteen year old, and - like his uncle and great grandfather - was recognised as brilliant in the scientific fields, so I figured he was the best one to approach for an opinion.

"Oh dear, whatever you do, don't go around saying Astrology is a science, or you might embarrass yourself", he advised in his serious way.

"Why not? Astrologers seem to think it is."

"Well, it's not."

"Why not?" I persisted.

"Because you can't prove it," Simon said blandly.

"So, the fact that it works is not proof enough?"

"Hmmm - that's open to conjecture anyway," he replied, sceptically. "Just because some people think it works doesn't make it true. To prove something you have to repeat an identical experiment many times, with identical results."

"Well?", I frowned at him. Simon looked at me as if I couldn't be more ignorant.

"How can anyone say Astrology is a science, when it examines moments in time? Each moment of time is different, so you can't possibly prove it."

"But it works!" I repeated.

"So you say, but it's not a science. It's a theory, that's all. And it's a concept you cannot prove."

He smiled knowingly, and dismissed me in his teenage way by turning back to his books.

18 RETURN OF HISTORY

By the time of our divorce, the fashion shops and coffee bar had been sold and no longer afforded an income, so - just as before - not having the least idea of how I was going to support my boys and myself, I launched once again into a completely different world.

Strangely, In spite of the principles behind our separation, Stuart and I never parted in spirit, for he continued to offer a distant hand of advice and support. To this day I will always think of him, as a genuine and much loved friend. We did connect up again a few years later, and his marriage to Marilyn did end in divorce as expected, but the moment had passed, and we very rarely socialised together after that.

Marilyn went on to marry a third time. Her husband was younger than her, and extremely rich, so it seemed her future would finally be calmer and more secure. They had nannies for the three younger children, extravagant dinner parties, socialised a great deal, and took long exorbitant holidays abroad, but in spite of all this, the relationship once again was not to last.

I always felt she was greatly saddened by the hand she was dealt in life, and didn't seem to know how to pull herself out of it. She was never really happy and often misunderstood, for she portrayed herself outwardly as rather a snob - aloof and distant, with a queenly attitude, and somewhat selfish - yet in truth she was a magnetic, fascinating individual that very few friends really got to know.

Over the ups and downs of the years that followed, we still shared a great deal together, and although I did find and mix with more of "my kind of people", as she put it, I don't think she has ever been able to live in her sort of world, without having to pay an awesome emotional price.

****

Whilst in the throws of recovery, I somehow managed to mortgage a large, rambling, and rundown place on the edge of town, which I filled with second hand furniture and decorated with bright oddments of leftover paint.

It is amazing what you can discover when money is scarce. I cut mouth-watering photographs of wholesome meals out of old magazines, and pasted them all over the kitchen walls, before doing the same thing in the bathroom with articles taken from the local Evening News. Finally, I coated everything with clear varnish. It lasted for years! Then, in order to survive the onslaught of costs whilst accommodating everyone, the house became full of lodgers, and friends of Sandy.

Sandy had returned to live with us again after her own long standing relationship failed and, complete with nightmares plus a lorry load of plants, she descended into the downstairs front room to re-awaken the return of history.

So there we were, all together once again - plus a couple of Arabs, a few stray students, two adopted cats, and a posse of pale-faced vegetarians, who roamed around in the afternoons, making enormous batches of lentil 'variations'. And then there were some guitar players who passed through residence, strumming away in the moonlit hours in vain competition with Sandy's magnificent stereo downstairs, and Matthew's pop music upstairs.

During the many contradictory episodes that followed, I was to learn more about myself, life, and other forms of 'reality', than I had hitherto even begun to explore. I was indeed a novice in another new field, and realised more and more that we all continue to be mere infants, stumbling along the precarious path of understanding.

It is true that the decision I had made all those years ago, after visiting my mother in hospital, was to lead me along avenues that on many occasions appeared to be dead ends. It is true that when, in my ignorance, I started out to find the border line between reality and illusion, I had no concept of the enormity of what I was attempting to do, but it is also true that I was aided and supported by some unknown force through it all, and many of the apparent dead ends and obstructions were necessary hurdles for growth and development.

All the pieces of information I had been given over the years were gradually slipping into their rightful places in my mind, and for me Astrology was the central pivot around which it all revolved.

As I had hoped, the subject had taught me about myself – the less obvious but real truth, with all its talents and inadequacies. Up until that point I hardly knew myself and, just as Stuart had declared, there were things I was not seeing that were repetitive cycles, which were definitely restricting my life.

For the following five years I threw myself into almost total seclusion, studying, examining, testing and finally believing that here at last I had found one bridge that could be used to travel safely across from the 'reality' of this world, to the so called 'illusion' of seeing things from an equally real, but much wider angle.

I remained out of contact with my brothers, and hardly saw my parents at all then, for in spite of my father's general tolerance, he couldn't accept my failure to make a success of yet another marriage. He was cross the first time, and decidedly cool for a while afterwards. As I've said before, he came from the era that really believed women and mothers had certain allotted duties to perform, which precluded divorce. But I also feel that, having stayed with my mother during the worst of times, he was unable to condone how I could so easily '*wander off into ridiculous pursuits'* as he put it.

I did do his chart for him once, but he wasn't very tactful about it, and suggested that my analysis was really nothing like him at all. He also expressly advised against me doing the same for my mother, for he felt certain it would disrupt her. So that was that - for the moment anyway.

The world continued amongst the trials of everyday life, and the hazards of bringing up two fine-looking adolescent lads - tall, blonde and strong - whom were both highly reactive and powerful in personality. Their size and stance often reminded people of Phil and Grant from the BBC soap at the time, although Simon now, would probably be mortified at the thought.

Life was hard on my boys, for they resented the fact that the house was awash with invaders, and I can't say I blame them, but it was the only way we could survive at the time. There was no other form of support, physically or financially, and being teenagers they had far greater needs than before. Although brothers and very close in age, they were, and still are, entirely different in personality, and each reacted to the situation in their own indomitable way.

My first born, took his studies very seriously, and had thrown himself into his work with the same intensity as myself.

Simon is a very old, special soul, and I have always felt there are two sides to him – the outdoor sporting type, who longed for the freedom of the sea, distant travel, and a more relaxed, continental environment - versus the book loving, ambitious, clever professor, intent on working very hard and making a good career for himself.

He had always shown a great propensity for scientific subjects - particularly chemistry - and, amongst other things, took up the study of German, for he spawned a great love for the country and its way of life. He studied continuously for many years, and is now a successful Patent Attorney.

However, at that moment in time, his exams were looming heavy on the horizon, and the strain of the constant battle with his books was beginning to show.

Matt (he objected to the name Matthew) was opposite in outlook. Although very loving and caring in nature, with the same intelligence as Simon, he looked on the world as a playground of comedy. He considered study and exams more than boring, and never reacted well to that form of discipline.

Whilst growing up, his main interest was in honing his football skills, and he even had trials for Arsenal once. However, later, he much preferred to hang out with his mates, or one of the many girlfriends he seemed to attract.

I have often felt that Matt should have become a car mechanic for he showed a great interest in making them into magnificent objects since very young. Being naturally very creative, he eventually became a Gas Engineer, and used his exceptional talent in the building trade.

Nevertheless, in his youth he loved designer clothes; hankered after the rich life, and revelled in fun and amusement - which turned out to be particularly difficult for Simon, as he became a prime target to be teased.

So, true to Newton's theory, the force of the opposites reacted to each other; something went wrong with the wiring, and chaos reigned in the house. Simon complained extremely loudly, which didn't help the noise, but he was trying to work in impossible circumstances, and when Matthew started his 'Trials

Bike' up in the kitchen at midnight once, because it was "raining outside" I really felt that Simon had got a point!

But we struggled on, and I certainly wonder at times how Simon managed to achieve so much during those years. Both of us disappeared into our rooms and rarely came out except for me to prepare meals, and them to eat, but even that became a major hazard, for whenever Matt and Simon crossed paths, there could be heard a series of thumps and scuffles, followed by,

"Boffin!"

"Moron!"

"Pocket Dictionary!"

"Ignoramus!"

Another time, I wandered out of my room to come face to face with a strange bearded man standing on the landing, who announced rather rudely,

"Who are you?"

"It's my house!" I replied indignantly. "Who are you?"

He ignored my question and continued, "Oh yes, I've heard about you! You're the woman who lives in the room upstairs",which just indicated how rarely people ever saw me!

It all got a little bit trying in the end, especially when Matt's sense of humour propelled him to pretend he was Simon, and one day started a long conversation with a child named Robert who was playing in the garden next door.

Matt couldn't be seen, as he was talking through the slatted window in the upstairs bathroom, and four year old Robert was enthralled with the chat from this disembodied voice named Simon, who told him that whenever he called out, he would come to the window again and talk to him. Of course the outcome can be well imagined, and poor Simon suffered massive daily disruption as a result, although we all laugh about it now.

I have to say it was extremely difficult for me too during those times for, with virtually no money and attempting to study myself, I also had to try to bring some sort of discipline into the place whilst all these activities were going on, and I assure you it was no mean feat. Very rapidly I became known as 'Dragon Woman' to the rest of the household, and all their visiting friends.

Nevertheless, having grown up with the strange and difficult situations of my own childhood, there was always part of me that tended, like Matt, to make a comedy out of the most horrendous situations, and that was the saving grace - plus John of course - for all through the pacing and theories and discoveries, there he was walking beside us all, light as a feather in his own special world full of fun.

19 "THE JOHN"

From the time that Stuart and I had parted in those weeks after the break up of my marriage, John had become my staunch ally and supporter. In many ways we had been thrown into each other's lives through force of circumstance, but, as it turned out, there was much more to it than that.

The first time I met John, I was struck by recognition. It didn't creep up on me as it had done with Eric and Stuart, but it was an immediate reaction, and I knew him as someone who had been close before, but in another time and another place. It was obvious that Marilyn had recognised him too - maybe as a distant lover of her past - and the head-on deadlock of John and Stuart at first meeting was as powerful as were the consequences.

Many have argued since that it was the circumstances that created such a major impact, and possibly that's true, but knowing and understanding the forces of Karma as I do now, there is no normal logic or reasoning that explains our inability to disentangle ourselves from the interlink of relationships that still haunts us today.

John initially moved in as one of the host of lodgers in the new house. It wasn't planned to happen that way, but there were a series of other issues, revolving around his ex-wife and children that left him without a home - so it became the obvious thing for him to do. He only stayed for a while until he was able to buy his own place – a more tranquil flat on the sea front, with wonderful views across the Solent, but I suppose it was inevitable that everyone would think we were in the midst of an affair, which caused a lot of very hurtful and unpleasant problems at the time.

John had a greatly loved dog, named Harvey, who

missed him so much that he followed his scent for miles to find him. One evening after John moved in, we heard a loud scratching at the door, and there was Harvey, covered in mud, with tail wagging furiously and a joyous expression on his face. John wanted him to stay, but knew the children would miss him if he didn't go back, and unfortunately he never came again. We discovered later that, after hearing about the visit, his ex-wife had sent Harvey to live some distance away from the family.

It was actually eighteen months later that John and I did commit to a relationship, which I suspect was also inevitable. Over the next five years, he not only became everything to me, but also filled the vacant male role model that my two sons seriously needed. Adrian was never really born to be a productive father figure, and neither was David, which was one of the reasons why the marriages ended. However John believed that "family" was everything, and being denied the closeness of his own children, he proceeded to extend his values to mine.

Simon, I feel, was confused by the whole process, because – as he told me later – he could never quite handle the unpredictability of our ever changing circumstance, which I think he found particularly hard. However, Matt rapidly responded to John's fun loving nature, and looked on him as not only a real father figure, but also someone he would always seek to emulate.

John was a true Londoner – born and bred within the sound of Bow Bells. He was the only son of Lily, a bright, petite little lady, and Maurie, his Jewish stepfather, who was almost overwhelming in his generosity. Lily used to remind me of Peggy, the Queen Vic character, for she was very similar in temperament and mannerisms.

As a child, John and his sister June grew up on the

rougher side of the city, with all that poverty entails. He told me once that his school days were sparse - for truancy was all part of the game of "ducking and diving" that he learned on the London streets. He felt that his best education was in the "ways of the world", and always recalled them as happy days, that had given him a healthy grounding for the future. However, his life had now changed considerably, and he felt very grateful to be able to afford the wonderful luxury of living by the sea.

John didn't fit with the classic style of good looks, but his indomitable presence and striking blue eyes gave him a magical intensity and strong magnetic appeal. It is no exaggeration to say that most men greatly admired him, and women easily fell in love with this East End boy – whilst both children and animals seemed to follow his lead as if he was the Pied Piper. He was a lovable, vibrant cockney, with a mane of thick blonde hair, and the physique and pride of a benevolent lion. However, in spite of his normal casual stride, brimming with confidence and humour, people were left in no doubt that he would brook no interference if forced to protect his territory.

Whilst working the local markets, John inherited two young brothers – barrow boys, named Freddie and Bobbie – who had the makings and response of Titans, even at the age of twelve. They were very congenial lads; challenging in height, with enormous limbs, and could pick up a twenty-pound bag of equipment in one hand, whilst moving it about as if it was a carton of milk. Every week without fail our house got a delivery of meat and vegetables in a huge sack of potatoes clutched in one Herculean fist. John inevitably followed behind, grinning widely and pointing at their hands, mouthing, "Clock the Forks! Look at the Forks!" - which highly amused us all.

So that was John – or "*The* John" as he came to be known. If ever Stuart was the 'Seeker of Truth', then

John was the 'Essence of Being'. Life to him was a playground of fun, comedy and laughter. He was a child of the Sun, the teenager of the Zodiac, and the King of the animal world. I know that Matt, particularly, was very proud to think of him as his surrogate father, and many were the teenage boys that looked on him as a role model, to be regarded with awed respect - especially as rumour had it that he had gone to the same school as the Cray twins. I never managed to find out whether this was actually true or not, nor who had originally spawned the idea.

Maybe it was John's instinct for survival; maybe it was his appreciation for the naturalness of his surroundings when he moved to this part of the country, but whatever it was, it gave him the edge on many of us who were struggling with our theories and intellectual viewpoints.

****

In the early days, I often wondered whether it was possible for John to be serious. We hardly discussed the things I was doing at the start of our association, for he said that I always surrounded myself with 'doom and gloom merchants' as he put it, and when I was with him, it was time for laughter.

But, after a while he started to push me to talk about my mother, my aims and my hopes for the future. He explained that, having been brought up with a Jewish stepfather, he believed – as Maurie did - that the mother figure was the most important person in the whole of any family, and regardless of the way they were, a mother always warranted attention and deep respect.

It was the first time this had happened to me in a relationship, for I honestly believe that both Adrian and David didn't look on my feelings as being a priority. It seemed to me that they both thought I was floating after an impossible dream that didn't merit much interest - for there were other more pressing and valuable things in life.   Much as it upset me sometimes, I could understand it really, because other people probably thought the same.

I suppose the most important thing for me, was at last I could to talk to someone that would listen, and take part sympathetically in sharing ideas, even if they couldn't understand.   I told him a lot about my experiences and the strange way things seemed to be coming together, but I still couldn't fathom out where it was all leading.   He didn't answer that question, of course, but he did tell me that I was concentrating too much on the "goal", when perhaps the greatest form of progress could be found right here in the earthly world around us. Thus he helped me to discover another aspect of reality, which still remains as one of the greatest joys of my life today.

John knew about nature. In spite of his lack of education he was obviously very quick minded and intelligent.   However, he wasn't the least bit interested in science, spiritual studies or 'The Stars at Night' as he used to call Astrology, but he had an uncanny unmentioned philosophy of his own, and that philosophy underlines earthly existence in its most natural form.

It is simplicity itself, for he felt the pulse of the animals, and walked in time with the seasons and, for the first time in my life, I found myself properly introduced to the mystery world of the elemental kingdoms. And there, under his direction that he created in the form of a game, I found myself moving back into the carefree make-believe world of my grandmother, and began to slowly re-discover the lost child in my nature, and the forces of 'other worlds' that shared our earthly existence.

A leaf wasn't a leaf to John. It was a 'miniature

being', whose sole reason for living was to enrich the world with enjoyment. Many was the time in the autumn, when the trees shed their canopies of red and gold across the pathways of the Common that ran down to the beach, I would find myself sprinting hand in hand with John, chased by a vast army of leaves that had been caught up and regimented behind us by a passing gust of wind.

"Quick! Quick!" John used to cry. "*They're forming ranks*! Get out of the way or they'll catch us! *Hurry!* They're coming!" And crazy as it might seem, it was quite automatic to run for out lives.

And then there were the birds, particularly the seagulls that used to duck and dive over the waves of the Solent. John knew all their moods and habits.

"Do you see that one?" He said to me one day, pointing to a wide-eyed, bedraggled looking gull. It was standing on one thin little leg whilst struggling to keep its balance in the wind.

"He was a Sergeant once, but lost his leg in the Seagull War. He's never been quite the same since..."

He seemed to have an uncanny knack of reaching into the life of animals, and particularly birds. Often they would swoop around him, as we walked along the beach, and even passers-by would stop in amazement. I remember one day he kept everyone fascinated as he took us all into a make believe world of Starfish space travel on nights of the full moon, and Crabs, gathering for afternoon picnics as they waited to admire the "Starling Fly Past" before the tide came in.

John lived life as if there was no tomorrow. He just loved being alive, and encompassed his "man's" world with exhilaration. He worked very hard; drank very heavily on his jaunts to the pub, and was challenged by nobody, when choosing to defend his position. With women and children, he was the dominant male - demanding, but exceedingly gentle, respectful and understanding of their needs – and above all he was immense fun.

John awoke the part of me that wished to 'play', and we used to have hilarious times 'attacking' the old castle ruins on the common, or lying flat and silent as statues in the long beach land grass, listening to the conversations of the people, who walked past quite unaware of our presence.

They were such good times, but not something I could keep pace with for too long, for it was really very exhausting, yet I loved John with all my heart and enjoyed every minute of his time.

And so as days went on I found myself able to look at life in an entirely new dimension. Through my studies I had learnt about the elementals - little miniature forces of fire, earth, air and water - that shared this planet Earth.

I had heard that the flame of the Salamander is just one flicker of the element of fire, just as the dew of the Undine is just one drop of the ocean of water: the breath of a Sylph is part of the wind and we all knew of the Gnomes from Irish folklore as the Little People of the earth, but I wasn't too sure if these little beings were actually *really* there.

Yet it was through John that I was able to truly appreciate them for the reality they were. Here was a make believe world that suddenly really came alive for me. It was no longer an illusion, for I could feel its presence and knew it existed. The world became alive - a vision of colour and quality - the Earth a living being, with sustenance, strength and form.

John hadn't read or even heard about the elementals, but he certainly knew them. It was he who taught me to welcome the sigh of silence in the whisperings of the night; seek out a face in the bark of a tree; touch the heartbeat of the rain as it danced on the windows; or drink in the shimmering warmth of the sun, and catch the scent of the wild wind, as it swept in billowing swirls at the edge of the sea.

It was he, in his innocent understanding of nature that could draw a welcome flame from a dying ember in the grate, and raise a flourishing plant from a drooping seedling in the earth. He'd been taught none of these things, yet instinctively knew them, and that was reality to me.

And so it was that I too found myself able to walk closer in time with nature: to recognise its message and to hear beneath the surface the vibrant pulse of life around us. There was so much I had missed in my questioning haste: so much glory and profusion of life, if only I had had the time and sensitivity to 'stand and stare'.

People may find it hard to understand how it is possible to fall so deeply in love with someone, yet have no desire to marry. John and I never did tie the knot, although he has definitely remained the greatest love of my life. He did ask me once, but we knew it wouldn't work. We were far too free in spirit to be tied again to the normal routine. In spite of eventually moving on, we never really separated – it was a pact between us that will last forever, for he is indeed my spiritual brother and my twin in fire.

I had a repetitive dream way back in my teenage days. It was a warm summer's afternoon, and I was walking alone through a beautiful park, when I came across a single ebony door - with the number 54 in golden letters carved upon it. Wishing to go inside, I cautiously turned the handle and opened the door - only to find there was nothing behind it but a lone graveyard. It was a terrible shock, and I was immediately struck by unutterable loneliness and grief. I never forgot that dream, for it often returned to haunt me, and each time the affect was quite devastating.

It was a sunny summer's afternoon in June 1997 when my John died. He was 54 years old.

20 WHEN IS A BODY NOT A BODY?

"The moment you doubt whether you can fly, you cease
forever to be able to do it."
J.M. Barrie - Peter Pan

From the day in 1976 when I first met John, to the day he died, was almost exactly twenty-one years. Quite a long time I suppose, but to me it seemed like just a moment, and looking back I am amazed how much change and learning came about in those short years. John met my parents just once, but that was only when they came on one of their very rare visits.

During those days, I felt my father had all but given up on me, for I don't think he could ever understand how my direction and thinking had swung so far into the "airy fairy" realms of imagination, which - after my mother - he didn't trust at all.

Dad was very pleasant to John, but I know rather regarded him as a passing phase. He once joked that, as I had travelled in relationships from public school boy, to policeman, to cockney market trader, he was next expecting me to turn up with a New Age priest, or a penniless musician. I didn't mind though, for my father was certainly not a snob. He just couldn't quite see where it was all leading, and since I had told him very little of the route I was trying to follow, it was quite reasonable to expect that he would be more than a little confused.

However, one thing was very apparent. It was through John that I was able to realise what true Freedom of Spirit meant, for it was his magic that had switched me away from the intense intellectual approach, and back to my Grandmother's world of fantasy and imagination – but it was not total fantasy, surely? Wasn't it just a different form of reality that maybe even I had tried to side step, because, like my father, and many others, I was still stubbornly standing on the side of logic, whilst trying to penetrate the wall of the inconceivable?

This thought opened doorways to move into the next phase, which couldn't be gleaned from books, or study, or anything at all but my Will, my Belief, my Faith, and the strength of my mind and imagination.

By this time, my mother seemed to be less and less conscious of the world around her. In the rare moments she was alone with me, she would sometimes make reference to her time as a child in India, and the traumas afterwards when they returned to Scotland. However, none of the stories were very coherent and it did seem as if she was going rapidly senile, or the drugs she was on had seriously destroyed her memory. I suppose, because I had the same birthday as her sister Joan, she often mistook me for her, and during those times became very cross, as if I had done something really bad.

The person she was very clear about, and seriously hated the most, was her stepmother, whom she repeatedly said had destroyed the family, for she really believed Doris was instrumental in the death of her mother. To me, this was very upsetting, because it wasn't clear if this was real or not, and I too seemed to be blamed for something in the past that I couldn't understand.

She gradually gave me more and more fragments of information, but never really got any nearer to saying just how and why my grandmother died. Every time I tried to pursue the question, Mum would go off on a complete tangent of upset and anger that always ended up anywhere but at the truth.

She told me once in her fury that, after her mother's death, her father had allowed "that woman" to melt down all of the beautiful jewellery meant for her and

Joan, and had it made into pendants and rings and luxuries for herself. Since my grandmother came from a very rich family, this must have been more than unfair. Mum was very bitter about it. She hated her stepmother with a vengeance, and eventually ran away from home at sixteen years old. She trained as a nurse, and it was through this that she met my father and married him when she was only nineteen.

I did actually write to Joan about these things once, and she did confirm that the jewellery had 'disappeared' but neatly evaded any further questions at the time. It was not until after my mother's death, that she eventually admitted that my grandfather didn't want the past "known" by the rest of the family - and this, she insisted, was in protection of Mum.

Unlike my father, my mother *was* a terrible snob - maybe because of her salubrious lineage perhaps? In the early days she was perfectly sure I would end up with a dustman, so I didn't expect her to take much notice of John. However, I was wrong. Like most people, she took to him immediately, and always asked about him afterwards, which she never did with Adrian or David. Many times she was insistent that the three of us had gone travelling together at night, and there was one occasion that she phoned me at 3am in the morning to ask us where we had got to, for she was just making a cup of tea and we vanished.

I remember we laughed about it at the time, but both of us knew that this story was perhaps not quite as crazy as it sounded. Sandy was always going "walkabouts" in the night, and John said he had often woken up to find himself floating in the air by the ceiling, and he did have some astoundingly life like dreams on occasions. One of these was to seriously shock us both.

It was about 2am in the morning when John phoned. I hadn't seen him that evening, and he had gone to bed early, only to wake up and find himself walking along the beach up by the castle ruins. He could hear two men talking angrily, and as he moved closer, he realised this was more than just a normal row. They were standing a little distance from each other, and one was holding a gun, whilst the other seemed to be pleading for his life.

John suddenly realised that the guy was about to shoot, and for some reason ran between the two yelling "NO!" just as the trigger was pulled. By all accounts he felt the bullet go straight through him, and he and the other man fell to the ground.

He lay there for a while, totally unable to move or say anything. The angry perpetrator ran over to them, but amazingly he ignored John, and - after peering closely at the other man - swiftly vanished into the darkness. Even more to his amazement John found he was completely uninjured when he eventually got up. Hurriedly he went over to try to help the young victim still lying on the ground, but realised immediately that the poor man was dead. It was whilst he was staring in confusion and shock, that he suddenly became aware that he was back in his bed.

"It was a terrible nightmare and so *real*, Babe," he said. "I had to down a good few bevvies before I rang you. I seriously thought the 'Ice-cream' had shot me, and I must be dead too!"

The next day we scanned the newspapers, but nobody had been found on the beach. However, there *was* a local youth who had vanished after a serious argument in one of the nightclubs on the seafront that evening - and was later found shot dead in another location. We were never quite sure if this was relevant or not. From his picture John said he thought it was the guy, and suggested that he had probably been moved somewhere else, but he absolutely refused to try to follow it up.

"Come on, Doll! Who wants to become the 'Nobble' of the century?" He quipped. "I do have my pride, already!"

****

The experience re-awakened my fascination with Astral Travel - or "Out of Body Experience", as it is known today. I was excited at the thought of being able to take active participation in my dreams. I had long since heard that it was a natural process which took place unconsciously whilst we slept, but it was rare that people remembered these experiences, and if they did they would put it down to just a dream.

I was past the point of being sceptical, especially after John's encounter, but other people didn't seem to have had such conclusive experiences - except Sandy of course, who was totally convinced that 'ghosts' were out there, waiting to take her to places where she didn't want to go.

By now my visualisation powers had become pretty good but, try as I would, I couldn't move either in or out of my body with any degree of certainty.

I did read books on how to do it, but eventually gave up trying, for I found myself up half the night, lying rigid and flat on my back, trying to imagine myself leaping out of lifts, or re-shaping my body to reappear way up on the ceiling - and the only result I got was utter exhaustion.

I suppose, it was because I gave up that it happened. It was a particularly fraught night, when the whole world had descended into the house and down into Sandy's room, and both Simon and Matt had decided to have a slanging match with a hippy on the landing around about two in the morning, before challenging each other to a duel of marmalade sandwiches on the stairs. The whole situation didn't seem at all funny at the time, particularly when shortly afterwards someone got locked in the loo, and had to hammer on the door loudly to get out.

I was lying in bed, feeling like a taut spring, and wondering what on earth I was doing having lodgers in the first place, when an extraordinary feeling came upon me. It was as if my whole body had been dislodged suddenly from its position, which was a totally new experience for me. I waited, rather expecting to have some psychic revelation or other, when I became aware of a massive inner vibration, and gradually I could feel the sensation of rising in the air, until I became level with the middle of the window on the opposite wall.

I felt very calm, which was lucky, for I was aware that any violent emotional reaction would have stopped the process, and everything would be lost. I waited, wondering what to expect, and found myself looking out through the glass, straight into the upstairs windows of the houses opposite. A woman in her dressing gown was drawing the curtains, and I was contemplating on what she might be doing so late at night, when my whole being did an abrupt about-turn and I found myself heading with force straight towards the opposite wall.

I ducked as an automatic reaction, but went straight through without feeling it, belted over the head of a sprawling sleeping guitar player, and straight through the wall at the back of the house. I couldn't believe it! There I was, floating about, swooping and diving like a bird over the tops of the houses, and completely conscious.

But, if I was in control of my mind, I certainly wasn't in control of my body. Within seconds I had spun into a tight circle and then, as if shot like a bullet from a cannon, I whizzed out into the universe, still buzzing like an angry bee towards the distant stars that I could see before me. There was a tremendous roaring noise in my ears, and a horrible smell of burning in my nostrils, which could only have come from the speed I was travelling.

I got so caught up in the sensation of movement, that I was only vaguely aware at first of the ground coming towards me at an incredible pace. As I came closer, I braced myself for impact, but there was no need, for I swept across the surface, and straight into the middle of a group of people gathered in the doorway of a large building.

"So you made it," I heard someone say. "We've been waiting for you. The party's about to start."

Still in awe, I went with them, through the archways and into the building, where there was indeed a party in its opening stages. It was great fun, and I knew everyone there, and they knew me.

I can still remember now, every feeling, every emotion and every communication of the moment, and also being concerned about getting back, for I had no idea how I had got there in the first place.

Everyone laughed when I asked, saying, *"Just follow the cracks in the Earth."* It was only the next morning that I thought what a strange statement that was, but it seemed perfectly logical then.

Off I flew, full of excitement at my new experience. The return home seemed slower. It was as if I was coming back on a long journey from a distant planet, and I remember seeing the beautiful blue green circle of the Earth growing larger before me. Then all at once I dropped like a Skylark out of the sky, and heading along, high above what seemed like a ravine deep in the earth, I felt myself floating down towards the house.

I landed in the larder in the kitchen, which didn't seem strange at the time, and, walking out through the wall, I met Sandy in the hallway. She was wearing a blond wig, and confided to me that she was using a disguise to 'avoid the ghosts', before she vanished through her bedroom door, and there I was, suddenly back in my room, vibrating about two feet above my body.

Once back in bed, I wasn't able to move directly, and I lay there trying to pull my thoughts together. Everything had been so utterly real, even down to the position of the tins of food in the larder. Surely I couldn't have dreamt those things?

I got up with burning excitement. How could I find out? I decided I would ask Sandy. She was lying flat on her face in bed, and I had to shake her awake.

I told her all about my adventure, while she sat there hugging her knees like a wide-eyed child listening to a fairy story.

"Did you meet a ghost?" she asked fearfully.

"No, *I told you*, it was a party, and I knew everyone, but don't know who they were now, which is really odd. I did meet you, though. You were wearing a blond wig."

"But I wouldn't be seen dead in a blond wig!"

"Well, I'm *sure* it was you. Don't you remember?"

"No, I don't!" she looked aghast.

"Oh well," I shrugged, disappointed   "I know it was real though. *I just know it!*"

It was four o'clock when I got back into bed. By now I was wide-awake, and wondering how all that could have taken place in such a short time? I mean, how could I have gone to another planet, had a party and come back again in less than two hours?

Undoubtedly, sceptics would say that this experience was just a vivid dream, but I often had vivid dreams, and this was nothing like it at all.

There was smell, and taste, and colour and sound; and amazing detail - like dust and cobwebs in the cavity walls as I passed though them, a nude lodger in the next bedroom with a discarded guitar lying across his legs, a tile missing on the roof of the house, *and* the position of the tins in the larder. Apart from the cavity walls I was able to check upon everything later, and none could be explained away.   I think it was then that I really appreciated that this wasn't a dream, but had actually happened, regardless of what anyone would say.

I drifted off to sleep still wondering, querying and arguing with myself, until daytime arrived in a flurry of activity.

Normally I would have allowed life to take over by concluding that the incident was just another one of many strange events, but this experience was set to stay - and I am now very glad - for I couldn't deny its' reality, or push it to the back of my mind.

21 THE POWER OF THOUGHT

From the time of that first "out of body" experience, I seemed to take a giant step forward in my awareness. I eventually became quite in tune with the repeated experiences, and found to my delight that I wasn't caught up in a series of unexplained or unconnected incidents. There was a definite purpose to my travels, and it was obviously necessary for me to consciously remember them, for it seemed that I was gradually coming under the tuition of 'something' far more advanced in understanding than myself.

I was shown places and associations that were all linked together with my long running search, and I learned to recognise the value of these encounters: taking the essence of their meaning, and relating them as much as I could, to everyday circumstances.

In spite of this, there was still the compulsion to find some discipline amongst these seemingly intangible incidents. It was as if I was trying to pluck a star out of the sky and bring it down to earth in order to examine it in the light of physical existence. So it was critical to always question - to check theories and other possibilities - if only to avoid becoming over credulous and start reading messages into perfectly simple events, which would have made the whole thing ludicrous.

If I had thought however, that my progress was going to lead me directly to the doorway of harmony, and finally to 'an answer', then I was severely mistaken for, in my determination to seek out my 'truth', I had misunderstood a vital principle that has caused many a disciple to fall by the wayside.

I hadn't understood the intricate forces of Karma at work and, in my urgency to speed up my spiritual development and destiny, I had failed to realise that, just as the force of electricity needs to be earthed for safety, so the lightning flash of enlightenment would seek to travel down through the planes and imbed itself firmly in physical existence in an attempt to obtain stability.

As fast as I was charging forth to increase my knowledge, so my emotional and physical life increased speed and momentum to try to keep pace alongside it. The resultant side effects led to unutterable chaos.

Sandy had abandoned Astrology not long after the course, for I don't think she really found any joy in it at all. Nevertheless, she was still continuing to follow her own avenues of discovery, which almost inevitably led her straight into the psychic fields again. At that time however, she had virtually no ability to discriminate between what was what, and those who *didn't know* seemed intent on pretending they *did*, and abusing her dreadfully by compounding her fears. True to her nature, she absorbed all atmospheres and opinions like a sponge, which left her in a constant state of exhaustion and irritability without any of us really understanding why, or how to help.

In the meantime, Simon was still valiantly contending with his studies, between various battles with Matthew's humour, wandering lodgers, and the unfortunate child, Robert, who lived next door.

Bit by bit, the whole household was slipping out of control, and I spent most of my time trying to keep the peace between grim, resentful undertones and vast shouting matches going on in strategic points of the house. Even the cats got offensive, and when I slipped on a pile of fat thrown by some idiot onto the garden path, I could have sworn one of them smirked as I sailed past.

Extraordinary things soon began to happen. I received a massive quarterly electric bill, which was ridiculous compared with the amount of fires we *weren't* using. When querying it, they insisted all was correct, but I didn't believe them, and after numerous checks they installed a second meter. Then astoundingly, I seemed to have developed the weirdest of uncontrolled powers.

If ever I became over tense, which was rapidly becoming most of the time, the T.V. or stereo would switch itself on without me being anywhere near the controls. I remember once having a confrontation with Sandy at midnight when music from her room suddenly blasted throughout the house. She insisted she'd never touched it, and since she was asleep when I stalked into her room, I really couldn't argue.

Eventually events got past the point of the ridiculous. Walls flashed precariously, lighting up the room when there was nothing wrong with the wiring. T.V.'s and stereos were blasting away at various intervals, and the repairs man was making almost weekly checks before he eventually told me to stop wasting his time.

I wouldn't have minded so much, but it was costing a fortune, and it wasn't as if anyone was conscious of making things happen. It was all completely erratic and quite unexpected. Yet it was strange that nobody was a bit frightened, not even Sandy who was normally frightened of everything.

We began to wonder if it was possible for those in the house - who were all under stress in one form or another - to have combined together to create this phenomenon through the power of their united thought? Or was it myself, or Sandy, or both of us? Or maybe even Simon or Matt, who were at the right age when poltergeists were often heard to activate? At the time of Angie's death, when the glass had smashed in the Village, the electrics had also played up in our house then.

Enough was enough, and something had to be done. After all, it wasn't exactly 'normal' to experience such things. People might be sceptical, but as far as we were concerned it had definitely become a reality, and getting more so, day by day. So with that in mind, I contacted a medium that had an excellent reputation. He was the principal of a local psychic foundation, and apparently an expert in this field. I am pleased I called, for I learnt a great deal through meeting him.

Tony was no ordinary medium, even though at first sight he looked a very ordinary chap. He seemed to me to be a "chipper" sort of man, who looked strangely similar to Andrew Lloyd Webber.   He was extremely 'down to earth', appearing rather set in his ways, and perhaps a little old fashioned, which was actually quite comforting, although there was no denying he had commanding personal power. As time went on, it was clear that underlying all the outward appearance, there was a strong Sherlock demeanour and intensity in his nature – complete with the pipe, love of good poetry, and somewhat obscure explanations.

When Tony entered the house, he confirmed my suspicion that the upheavals were due to disruptive energy rather than poltergeists or the like, but suggested that the emotional energies were completely out of balance, especially with Sandy's psychic traumas and two quite volatile teenage boys living there as well. He also added that I was extremely out of balance myself.

We talked for a long time.   As far as I was concerned, I felt very much in control of my mind and reactions, for surely the whole essence of my study was involved in learning the techniques of controlling such things?

Tony listened to me carefully, but shook his head, "You are in serious danger of over-polarisation," he said.

"Over-polarisation? What on earth's that?"

He contemplated for a minute, puffing on his pipe, before saying slowly,

"The world is in a continual state of change and adjustment to retain balance. You're telling me that you want to help your mother and others who are mentally sick, but *Balance* is the keyword.   It is essential to keep that balance, for without it we become absolutely no good to either ourselves or anyone else. When attempting to develop our mental and spiritual being, we must be very mindful of the fact that we have a physical being also which mustn't be neglected."

"But I don't neglect it." I interjected. "I can hardly do so in a household like this. The mundane world is all around me!"

"Hmm.... And phenomena...." Tony replied dryly, still puffing his pipe.

"Well, I can't help that...."

"Yes you can. Your attitude of mind is attracting things to you to try to retain balance.

"Like what?"

"Well, it's quite simple really," he explained, "Your constant investigations are taking you beyond the logic and into both the psychic and spiritual worlds. This has swung the pendulum too far in one direction. The obvious reaction is to force it back in the opposite direction in order to retain balance. Thus you become faced with two extremes of conditions.

"By obsessive concentration on these endeavours you've attracted the equivalent amount of force straight through your door and down onto the physical plane, which has produced the apparent peculiarities appearing in the house. The mind needs rest, by simply doing nothing or concentrating on lighter things. This helps to balance the energies. I guarantee you haven't been doing that, and hence your problems."

He knocked his pipe out in the ashtray before continuing,

"In this sort of work, there are *many* called, but *few* are chosen. The work of the 'psyche' is a perfectly natural process, which is the Birthright of us all. However, the public in general rarely look on it as "normal", and often mediums themselves have little concept of the meaning of balance, which can produce chaotic emotional conditions around them. That's how people fail, then take fright, and move away from the subject. Take my word for it, the root of success lies in the art of retaining balance amongst constant change."

I smiled to myself, and he looked at me quizzically.

"Oh, I was just thinking," I said. "The good old Law of Cause and Effect. It keeps cropping up everywhere."

"It's just a question of common sense really," Tony smiled, "We're all part of an intricate pattern which moves all the time."

"Yes, I know that, but so few people understand why things happen to them, or what they themselves can do about it. There appears to be plenty of critics but rarely anyone who is prepared to support and advise, without insisting that their own personal beliefs are always right for everyone. There are so many terrible fears about the unknown, which surely must cause half the trouble?"

I was aware my voice was raised in frustration, but continued anyway.

"I've had to blindly battle really hard to find anything out all on my own!   There are numerous things that people either fear or ridicule.   Many believe that Astrology is nonsense, and anything "non-provable" must be just a figment of a deluded mind.   If they bothered to investigate first - before dismissing out of hand - they might find that there *is* a reality and logic there, if only they looked properly with a less cynical eye.

"And logic, is that important?" asked Tony.

"Well, it *is* to me, and it *seems to be* to a million others."

Tony mused for a minute, "I think you'll find that people will see only what they want to see, and what is more, they will only see that when they are ready to see it."

"So, we just have to accept it and not even try to show them?"

"No, we don't have to accept anything, but we can waste a lot of energy by refusing to do so."

I looked at him for a minute, not agreeing at all. I couldn't accept it. If everyone did that there would be no progress at all, surely?

And what about Sandy? Tony had said that he felt she was so injured she was beyond help, and he couldn't do anything for her.   This really annoyed me, for if people like him - who *trained* potential psychics - could not see a way to help her, then what was it all about?   Surely there must be someone who could show her how to handle her fears or balance her psychic energies so she wouldn't be faced with these awful traumas?

And what about my mother too, and the dreadful

172

things she was forced to deal with? She had obviously recognised something in Sandy that was very akin to herself.   Was Sandy then, to be abandoned as a hopeless case, just like my mother?

I felt my hackles rise even more.   All these things were never discussed in public but shoved under the carpet along with vague warnings and preconceived judgements – maybe for fear of contamination perhaps?   That was no good to anybody. Didn't we all need to be educated about life, as well as other things?   And how could we ever freely express ourselves when considered 'peculiar' if we had powers that others couldn't understand?

Nobody explained - why not?   Why was it all such a secret?   I looked up fiercely as Tony watched me.

"Why are those in the 'know', so covetous of their knowledge?" I accused.

"Are they?" said Tony. "I don't think that's possible. Knowledge is universal. It belongs to everyone."

"So no-one has the right to hold onto it?"

"No, but nobody can hold onto it. It's all there in front of us if we care to look."

"But there must be some who are more capable of showing the way?" I persisted. "Why don't they do it?"

"Well, of course they do! They're doing it all the time, but we have to *recognise* a teacher before we can learn from them…and we have to recognise we *are* a teacher before we can teach!"

He got up, and started to pull on his coat as he moved to go – before tapping his head and adding pointedly,

"Listen to your mind! Learn to recognise and follow the signs."

And so it was that this man, quite unexpectedly, set me on a teaching path that laid the foundations for my own school. It began with one course in Astrology that never ended.

22 DIAMONDS IN THE CROWN

Once again I became involved in yet another direction, but this time it was as if I had finally reached a highpoint of discovery. I hadn't thought of teaching before, but it was to become a vital factor of research as it gave a platform to test a multitude of theories, and certainly proved invaluable in the future.

Tony set me up with the first class of 32 friendly but expectant adults, all of whom were already interested in the less scientific approach to life – a captive audience one could say. However, to me, the idea of taking command of this group was initially as terrifying as entering a room of shifty lions!

They say a teacher learns from their students, and this is certainly true. Indeed, it was through their continued questioning scepticism, that I was challenged to explain things with more than a modicum of common sense and logic. Often the queries led on from Astrology and into other more intangible areas. It is one thing to resolve this for oneself, but quite another to give productive information to people - who may be of like mind - but certainly have very different ways of thinking and finding understanding.

Very surprisingly I did find answers though – both for them and myself – and also to some of the more complex questions that I had never even thought about before. At first this seemed very strange, for I sometimes gave replies that I didn't even know I knew.

I learned after a while, that if I went to sleep requesting some information that had hitherto eluded my normal searching, I would almost certainly find the answer through an astral experience, dream state, telephone call, or a book that was handed to me the following day.

In this way, many realistic solutions were obtained,

and although very aware of the danger of giving credence to unexplained "voices", I became more and more open to the many 'telepathic' forms of communications received, which infiltrated as somewhat profound thoughts in my mind. These gave such important insights into seemingly impossible questions, that I came to seriously listen and trust their accuracy, for the information was always found to be true, and definitely far superior to my own knowledge and wisdom.

There were hard times too. Sometimes, it was as if I was interacting with others over incredible distances just by a "thought", but also discovered that if I became too fretful over a puzzle, then there would be long phases of inability to make any sort of connection, which left me both frustrated and very upset. It was as if the links I had worked so hard to find were deliberately cut, and I found myself suspended in chronic isolation.

Added to the dilemma, there was another problem. As close as I felt I was getting to an important answer - or at least some explanation and maybe help for my mother and her desperate unhappiness - the further I felt removed from my family. It was as if a doorway had opened to a wondrous new world for me, but another had firmly closed on their kind of world at the same time.

The more I discovered, the less I was able to communicate with my father or my brothers, except in the everyday sense. If I tried rather weakly to explain my thoughts, they were politely but rapidly dismissed as strange and impractical in the "real" world, and I became very aware that these "outlandish" ideas must have appeared to them as crazy as my mother's. It was therefore easier to just chortle along in a bright sunny way on the very rare times I saw them.

So, in spite of my excitement, I found those times of

loneliness terrible, for my sensitivity was increasing with understanding, and I became far more insecure and unsure of my footing with every step along the way.   The more I learned, the more I realised I knew nothing at all, and when it seemed that support was withdrawn, the sense of total inadequacy was almost unbearable.

And yet there were other times, when I had caught onto an idea or proved something to myself which was a major achievement, leaving me feeling overwhelmed with enthusiasm and joy; spurring me forward to new and wider fields of endeavour.

It was during one of these better phases that I came across what I felt were truly the Diamonds in the Crown. It was two things really. One being that I finally started to understand the wider basics of how the mind actually works - which I truly believe is still not yet recognised, or accepted, by doctors and scientists of today. And the other being that this realisation - and everything I had learned over the years - constantly returned me back to the Qabalah, and the profound Wisdom of The Tree of Life.

Through my study I had become aware that there was far more to the mind than just the functions of the brain. Of course this organ of thought and feeling had been demonstrated to house *conscious* intelligence, as well as *subconscious* memories et cetera.   Yet, even through all the advancements of the present day, science still seems to think that those "little grey cells" express the totality of the human mind. However others believed, and still do, that the *super-conscious* is also intrinsically part of us, but not associated with the brain at all, for it is the mind of the soul, and remains functioning after death.

So I knew about these areas of the mind, and believed in them all, but never could fathom out exactly how they all worked together, and what actually went wrong when they didn't.

"You might understand that the mind is a combination of three sections that work together, but you don't understand how thought evolves, which is the key to it all." Tony said, challenging me to look at things from a different perspective.

"So why are thoughts so important?"

"Because thoughts should travel through each part of the mind in sequence – We live life first through *conscious* experience; then as a *subconscious* memory of that experience; and finally the *soul-mind's* objective observation of that experience, which is passed back down the line as 'understanding' – that is the correct order – *conscious, subconscious* and then *super-conscious*. It's like a long tunnel, with thoughts from each experience going to and fro like traffic".

"That means the subconscious is right in the middle?"

"Exactly, and that is where the trouble can start - you can't order the mind to behave itself, because the subconscious is the most active part. It stores the memories, and doesn't think in words, it thinks in pictures, so we have to learn to speak to it in pictures."

I was silent, appreciating what he was saying. Strongly emotional experiences created extremely dynamic pictures, both good and bad, and visual impressions were always more powerful than any words.

"So these emotional images can get stuck in the subconscious?"

"Yes! Thoughts don't *belong* to us any more than traffic belongs to a tunnel. They should continually pass through and out the other side, like a constant flow, moving both ways." He paused for a moment, puffing on his pipe as usual.

"Thoughts should be as free as the air we breath, yet many people systematically cling onto bad memories - maybe in the form of hate, fear, grief or obsession of any sort."

"And that could create a blockage which will get bigger and more confused as other thoughts pile in – just like a jack-knifed lorry in the centre of a tunnel?"

"Exactly!" he replied, laughing, "*Now* you get the picture!"

I suddenly felt very depressed. How arrogant I had been for not fully appreciating just how difficult it must be for doctors to sort the blockages found in mental and emotional illness.   It was all very well understanding how or why such problems could arise, but learning how to deal with it and finding a long lasting solution was quite another matter.

Nevertheless, it seemed even more obvious that drugs and other forms of pacifying treatments only put a blanket over the traffic jam of pain, and did nothing to unravel it. Psychology and psychiatric treatments must help, but just talking surely couldn't really make the difference if people couldn't understand themselves and what actually made them tick?

Obviously the memory of what had happened to my mother had stuck in her mind – that thought; that image of pain; that tragedy. And over the years other events and frightening things had continued to compound the issue, so in the end nothing could get through. Drugs may submerge the subconscious, but don't hold back or clear the memory.

I really felt very inadequate. In spite of years of study, I didn't have the qualifications or understanding to help those already ill, but I did have the experience and knowledge maybe to help prevent things happening for others? And this is when I realised the true value of an ancient teaching that was to become the other diamond in the crown.

All through the years, after that meeting in the dusty bookshop in Golders Green, I had never given up in my eagerness to really try to understand the Tree of Life. However, it was not until I stumbled across the more western approach to the subject, that things became much clearer.

A friend of mine introduced me to the works of Dion Fortune, the author of The Mystical Qabalah, and founder of a Hermetic Order known as the Inner Light. Although I never took up the study of the subject, the various things I came across during that initial reading gave me a deeply fascinating and basic platform from which I could do my own investigation.

The Tree of Life - the principal tool of the Qabalah* - is often described as a map of potential and opportunity. A passage of experience, that leads us from our most basic physical self to the heights of our spirituality – with all the numerous turnings and pathways of discovery on the way.

If you can imagine, it was like coming across a secret treasure chest of unknown and fascinating promises. A sacred cabinet of magical drawers, full of exciting folders – each one dedicated to a different aspect, personal to ourselves, but *also* to the world, the universe, and everything around us. To me, this was something I had been waiting for – a way to access the many different facets of the mind, and most particularly, the subconscious.

It has been stated that there is never a voice so strong as that of the converted, and, yes this must be said of myself. However, I would challenge those who have seriously investigated this subject, to disregard its value as a psychological tool of self- understanding.

I would like to say that 1979 was the year when it all started, but of course it didn't because the real beginning was over 35 years before. However it *was* right then when the light of sudden understanding flashed in my mind and heart, and I knew that – at least for me – here at last were two very profound answers to the eternal questions that had always haunted my life.

23 GAINS

My very dear grandmother had, and still has, a profound affect on me, and I have spent most of my life following her ideals.   She is one of the people I have missed most since she died, yet also gives me the strongest feeling that she is still around.

As I have said, the wonderful thing about her was that she was exceptionally unusual for her time.   Her greatest gift to a child was to open the door of imagination in such a way as to bring the magic and wonder of life, even into otherwise difficult and desperate situations.   She believed in the sense of living by certain rules, but not being dominated by them, and if any became too demanding or rigid, to have the courage to change them.

She also held an infinite belief in the wisdom of Rudyard Kipling's "If" poem, and often said that if we weren't able to do anything else, we could at least attempt to follow its' guidance.   This is always something that has worked for me, and I was to try to follow this advice often in the following years, for it was a time of great excitement and gain, but also one of serious loss.

In the beginning, after some persuasion, Sandy had agreed to come along to classes with me for moral support. This actually turned out very opportune, for although she has always remained exceptionally sensitive, she found that through the more analytical yet visual approach to astrology, the dreams began to subside.

It wasn't long before she joined a further group, and eventually turned out to be an exceptional teacher, for the enormity of her imagination became her greatest asset.   Many is the time I have seen her with arms akimbo in dramatic illustration of the intensity of

Scorpio, the martyrdom of Capricorn, or the peculiarities of other signs, leaving everyone enthralled and alive with the images she portrayed. This gave me great joy, for I'd been with her from the nightmares of her subconscious right through to the re-birth of herself.

In latter years, she now remains one of the best astrology and tarot counsellors of the present day.

My classes continued on, from astrology into tarot, karma, visualisation, and beyond. One rapidly followed the other, for word had got around and they had become very popular with this more unusual way of teaching by visual description. Thus, I found myself almost running in front of my students, extending and consolidating previous courses, whilst creating something new.

So before I knew it I was teaching 7 days a week, and telling everyone stories of my grandmother and the day of the purple hat – just as she had predicted!

Two years later, in July 1981 I founded my own organisation. It was named Maat – after the Egyptian Goddess of Truth and Justice; a "Self-help", and later "Mystery" school that ran for over 25 years, to become the forerunner for The Order of the White Lion today.

It was not that I wanted to leave the psychic foundation, for I continued to rent rooms for a short while after, and I have always believed we have remained linked in someway. However, I felt my direction was different, and there was so much more that I needed to experience and teach, in order to extend into other fields of endeavour.

For me, the symbol of Maat represented everything to do with the fine balance needed to encourage the co-existence of all beliefs, whatever race, culture, or creed. It was not about one trying to convert the other, but about everyone working together - side by side in harmony - in the common search for the One Universal Truth that ensured peace of mind.

This was a tall order I know, but even if it only promoted the growth of public interest in the art of self understanding, and enabled people to find the freedom to help themselves, and tolerate others more easily, it was worth it to me.

It was great, for many people I knew joined - including Marilyn, and later a mutual friend Jenny - a bright, wonderfully cheerful person – very pretty, with cropped blonde hair, and a happy open expression. She had a great sense of humour, and there was a gentle purity and innocence in outlook, that likened her to the young Doris Day or the legendary girl next door.

When Jenny came I was both flattered and amazed, for her life was so worldly I doubted she would stay. She wasn't easy to read, and the mathematical mechanics of astrology were not exactly her forte, so, much to her amusement, I found myself repeatedly asking if she would ever come again. However, both she and Marilyn seemed to gain a lot of insight about themselves, which led them into more advanced courses. Both remained for a number of years and, although Marilyn wasn't able to stay for the final year, Jenny remained, and is still with us today.

In 1983, I had sold my previous place and bought a more compact terraced house in a street called Gains Road, which seemed fortuitous at the time, although in the end it didn't quite live up to its' name. Later I discovered it was ironically situated between two religious factions. A Born Again Christian Soldier of God's Army lived on one side, and the previous headmaster of the boys' junior school - now an ex Catholic monk - lived on the other.

I took this to "*mean*" something, but I never found out what.

The house wasn't very big, but had a compact little flatlet on the ground floor at the back, which became Matt's personal domain. Simon was away taking his degree in Chemistry at university, and I lived upstairs amongst varying bits of furniture; visiting students; Winston, a neighbour's black cat who decided to move in; and Maria – an ash blonde, white-faced lodger, with matching clothes – whose phantom image roamed around silently, terrifying anyone who suddenly came across her.

"*My God,* that was a fright I had!" announced John, as he called in to see me one evening. "I've just met a ghost on the landing!"

I don't know why but the house didn't inspire me much. I never moved in emotionally, which is lucky really, as it was not too long before it was time to move out.

After two further years, things had expanded so quickly that we began opening classes across the South of England, with Sandy and a few others now starting to teach the beginners. Our name became quite well known, and I felt really grateful that the teaching format was not only fun and exciting, but particularly helpful for those who were really struggling to find their way in often impossible circumstances.

Nevertheless, in spite of this achievement sadness beset me, for, having forged through the everlasting questions, and finally come to some of the answers, it seemed time had run out for my mother. After all, she was the one that had pointed me in the direction of my destiny in the first place. How ironical that this wouldn't apply to her, when it was started for her. Yet, I suppose it wasn't realistically possible to ask my father to change his approach towards her treatment, or trust so immediately in the value of my beliefs, when it had taken me all these years to trust them myself.

It was a strange time, and didn't seem as if it was going anywhere really. There were lots of students, lots of work, lots of fun and laughter, but certainly no glitter. In fact I resigned myself to looking more like a scarecrow most of the time.

Luckily Viv and Ruth – two strong supporters - helped me greatly with administration, but the workload certainly took its toll.

Viv had been with us from the beginning, and was one of the first teachers, along with Sandy. She was a comforting, forthright person, who worked full time in a charity shop. Being very loyal, quiet and unassuming, she strongly cared about the importance of "duty", which unfortunately left her trapped and frustrated at times, for she was secretly quite a rebel at heart.

In contrast Ruth was a more recent convert - an alert young woman about town, employed in an important position in a high-powered company. She was always smartly dressed and very conscious of everything being in its' rightful place - indeed, a perfectionist in the ways of business and the world. However, her heart wasn't really there, and she soon let go of the façade of her job, which seemed to give her great relief.

Meeting early one morning to try to clear the backlog of photocopying, we looked a motley crew, for Viv was suffering from the residue of flu, Ruth complained she hadn't slept all night, and I had a hangover. We were all dressed like flunkies.

So it was unfortunate that Marilyn chose that day to bring her friend Pat along, with a view to attending classes as she was having serious problems in her life. Looking stunningly arrayed in immaculate clothes, hair beautifully brushed, and faces aglow with red lipstick, they tripped into the room, their high heels clicking loudly on the bare floor.

Pat was obviously doubtful, so I decided to hold back, as I didn't believe in pushing anyone. But after a while, Ruth - unable to contain her newfound eagerness – stepped forward encouragingly.

"You know I used to be like you, wearing trendy clothes, make up, and high heels all the time" She enthused, before spreading her arms out in a gesture of glory. "But I joined the courses, and look at me *now!*"

In a moment of suspended silence Pat stared at her aghast. She glanced at Viv, then myself, with our strained ashen faces, before slowly shaking her head, and muttering defiantly,

"No... way!"

She never did come back!

****

And so yet another era dawned in unfolding the future, but it was a hard haul to deal with, and not without disappointment.

I was finding myself overrun with courses, and really struggling with how to handle the expansion efficiently, when a close associate suggested I should meet a competent business and promotion expert. Hence, I was introduced to a colleague of his, who was to completely redefine my approach, and soon became a major player in my life.

Ian was what I would call one of the beautiful people - gentle, yet magnetic, mysterious and intense. He was gay, mercurial in nature, and a social butterfly: always beautifully dressed in the fashion of the moment, and astoundingly generous towards everyone. In fact he took a multitude of risks with money. Nothing was beyond his imagination. He had so many fingers in so many pies it often brought him really close to the mark.

And luckily, or unluckily perhaps for both of us, he chose to see what could be done for Maat.

He was fascinated by everything, and gave the impression of being already aware, and even in tune with the sort of things I was doing. He seemed especially interested in the encounter I had with John Lennon. I had no intention of it happening, but astonishingly I really did make a very strong connection with Lennon after he died, and it was extremely valuable to me at the time - for the information given was not a personal message, but about more universal issues that gave me great insight and understanding of humanitarian concerns that I had not seriously considered before.

Because of Ian's obvious interest, and my honest belief in its' importance, I foolishly allowed this experience to be taken up by local newspaper. Shortly afterwards, I was confronted with the front page headline, dramatically stating "POMPEY ASTROLOGER GETS MESSAGE FROM THE GRAVE", which was absolutely horrifying, and left me in a state of acute disappointment and embarrassment for days.

Ian wanted me to make an impression on the media, because he said it was the only way that I would be able to expand and progress further. However, nobody appeared really interested in the reason behind the study, or its' purpose. They pursued information zealously, but with what seemed to me the intention of unveiling something far more sensational than sensible, and indeed far more "bonkers" than believable.

In the early days of aspiration, Ian spent a great deal of time and money in promotional effort, and I spent equal quantity of time in confusion and no little amount of fear, for the whole process totally freaked me out.

I appeared on TV and radio, but I just wasn't cut out for those sort of interviews, as they either wanted me to manifest a phenomena, or explain the answer to the universe in 3 minutes flat, which left me constantly having to suppress the urge to throttle them.

Yet, in spite of my misgivings, Ian was wonderful company and really believed in what he was doing, so together we forged a partnership, and both of us made every effort to make it a success.

Certainly his staff worked extremely hard. They were fascinated, and some even joined the courses. I think they saw plenty of humour in the proceedings, for I remember walking into Ian's office one day to see the following on the wall.

> "Don't speak to us of Pensions,
> In fact we have not any,
> We work for Ian until we're dead,
> And then we work for Jenni."

At that time I really did have high hopes for the future. The classes were going so well, and rather naïvely I believed that by becoming better known it would be a great help to laying the foundations for a worldwide form of teaching - and maybe, just maybe, my father and others would come to believe that what I was doing was really worthwhile.

24 LOSSES

In the early days of Maat, Terri joined the classes, and during the very short time she lived, she made a tremendous impact on us all.

If I was to put Terri and Jenny alongside each other, I would say they were mother and daughter – for not only were they very similar in demeanour, but both gentle, expectant, joyous in nature, and deeply affected by the beauty of the world. They were also both looking for something more substantial than the outward pleasures of life.

Terri always said that this was going to be *her* time. Her husband had retired from his position as top brass in the military, and they had exchanged their rather grand place for a cute little terraced cottage in the centre of Southsea.

When we met, I knew she was going to become important. She told me that she had seen me as a cameo image in a dream, which always happened with significant people to her. Being extremely interested in astrology, and particularly tarot as a form of self-knowledge, she loved the sessions, and very soon found herself deeply involved.

Regretfully during that time, I almost totally lost touch with my family as so much was happening all at once. Our lives changed completely in that year. Simon was still away at university; Matt soon mortgaged a comfortable flat in town, and I was transported into this momentous whirlwind of activity.

I have to admit I was more than a little in love with Ian. He was such great company – challenging, inspiring, deeply sensitive, and exceptionally creative. I certainly enjoyed spending time with his friends and partners – some of whom also joined the courses and stayed for many years. However, he was definitely a workaholic, and expected me to be the same.

When things started to progress so fast, I knew I couldn't possibly continue running everything, as well as doing what else was needed, so I would have to start receding from the "hands on" approach. As Terri had been there a while by then, and others didn't seem to relish the responsibility, I asked her to help with the running of Maat, and she willingly agreed.

We talked a great deal about the process, and I wrote a complete format for her and the teachers, with an outline on how to progress without so much of my input.

But - as is often true of the best laid plans - it wasn't to be.

It was a desperately sad moment when we discovered that Terri had cancer. She phoned me on a bright sunny day in autumn - one of those times when it seemed as if nothing could go wrong. We knew she had been unwell, but certainly nobody was prepared for the abrupt change of circumstance.

"I am dying", she said quietly.

"Oh, Terri…" I paused in shock "Are you sure?"

"Yes. The tests are positive, and it is terminal. It's all right; I'm okay about it. I just wish it wasn't happening so soon. I would so like to see the daffodils in spring once more, but they don't think I will last that long". She was beginning to cry quietly.

"I really don't want to leave this beautiful world".

So once again the tenacious grip of cancer systematically took its toll. Deeply saddened, I watched her going through the same pain and exhaustion as Angie before her, and she faced it all with the same immensity of courage. But she was not alone, for she had made so many friends, and we all took turns in being with her, trying to make it a little easier.

In the meantime, I was finding it harder and harder to keep up with the workload. Ian really tried, but I guess he was disappointed in me, for I wasn't able, or prepared, to promote myself in the way he wanted. He - as an expert in the publicity field – felt the input of a well-known personality would put us in a much better position.

So, when Yoko Ono was appearing in London, he arranged for us to go there. He hoped I might make an impression on her because of my previous experience. However, without introduction, this meant I had to casually leap up to her in front of the cameras. For someone like me who insisted on stubbornly waving the flag of integrity, the whole thing was obviously doomed to failure. To a promotional mind, this was just one way of getting noticed, but to mine it was both embarrassing and pretentious. Ian was not at all happy.

Nevertheless, we carried on trying to raise media awareness in other ways, and attempted many huge and impossible schemes. Ian believed in encompassing the 'bigger picture', and even began planning a huge international conference.

Michael Bentine – one of the well-known "four" that used to participate in the very famous "Goon Show" comedy of our younger days - phoned to talk about the meeting at 7am one morning. I mistook him for Matt doing one of his imitation voices, and responded by saying "Oh Yeah right!", whilst laughing loudly in disbelief. Luckily - being the ex "Goon" he was - Michael found it very amusing, but it really didn't do much to enhance our credibility.

Who knows, with the amount of effort Ian put in, it

might have worked – but again things were not to be, for fate overtook us as a harsh reminder of life.

With all the upheaval, big plans and on going classes, things rapidly started to slip out of my grasp. The result was that I lost my house - plus everything I owned - and landed back in this earthly world with a tremendous bump.

I wasn't able to pay the mortgage, you see. Although I had been a good businesswoman in the past, when dealing with spiritual concerns I was loathed to charge more than pittance for the sessions. After payments to the teachers, and hiring accommodation, the debts mounted, so in the end I was forced to sell Gains Road. Paradoxically, by then I owed £19,500, and received almost exactly that amount in profit – just enough to clear my debts.

So that was it. I had sold, and now had nothing. Luckily, Ian had an aunt who rented out rooms, and one was allocated for me. By then it was late autumn, and I don't really remember much about the place, except it seemed very dark and austere.

Sandy and her little mini helped me to move in. As far as I can remember, I had sold everything bar a few small pieces of furniture, so I only brought two chairs, and a bamboo screen. I don't remember much else, or even where the room was in the house - except I know it was in a long corridor on the left somewhere. There was a lavatory at the end, which looked and smelt as if it had given up the will to live.

The room was only small, about ten foot square, and housed a single bed, a sink, a cooker, and two kitchen cabinets. Sandy and I put the screen in front of the units, draping it with bright rainbow coloured throws, and we put more over the bed. With a few stray pictures, it took on a more homely look. Nevertheless it was very cold, and with no money, heating was a problem so I only went there to sleep in the evenings.

To get a bath was a major event. It was upstairs, and there was a 50p slot machine that enabled people to get hot water. The system banged loudly and took two hours to heat up, so if I didn't stand guard over it, some nameless apparition leapt in before I could get there.

A sharp-faced man, with the shock of black hair, haunted the corridor outside the room. His under nourished body stalked aimlessly through the passage each night, and since all the communal lights were on a timer, I kept seeing his dark Jack Frost shape suddenly illuminated by my lamp as it passed across the glass panel in my door.

I think Ian contacted my father. I know he wanted me to have support from my family, but Dad was really disappointed and angry at what he thought was my foolish behaviour. I was left no option but to properly explain everything to him, and why I had set about this in the first place. I sent him a tape, telling him all about my feelings and what I was trying so hard to do for Mum, but I have to confess I cried for most of the time.

My father sent me some money, and I never felt more alone.

I cut down all the classes, and receded back from a larger organisation to just holding a few sessions with me at the helm – the same way it had begun. Having done that, I actually didn't feel too bad, but nobody was happy I was in that room, especially John and my sons.

John suggested that maybe I should consider whether to continue, and wisely pointed out that people may not want to listen or believe in someone purporting to have the answer to life if they were living in the conditions that I found myself. I knew he was right, so I quietly put out a call to the heavens, asking for some sign to tell me what to do, and – if it was right to continue - I would find a way to provide a proper home; a place where I could both live, teach, and house my classes: a tall order, I know, but I had great faith in the power of entreaty.

If anyone really investigates their life they will probably find that whenever they have put out a sincere plea for help, it has come to them two-fold. It just needs to be recognised that's all, and interpreted in terms of what is actually *needed* rather than what we, in our wisdom, decide we *want*. Nevertheless, what happened next, was completely unexpected.

About a week later I went to visit Terri again. She was desperately ill and frail by then, but so pleased to see me. She carefully took my hand and whispered.

"As you know, I'm not going to get better, and I have made plans about my little house... I want you to have it. My husband doesn't want it, or the furniture, and I would so like you to move in after I go. Please do this, and make it a happy home full of laughter for me?"

I was deeply touched, and very shocked, for I had only put out the request such a short time before. I thanked her and said I was very grateful, but privately felt very uncertain and concerned, for it didn't seem right to benefit from her death. Anyway, it would probably be totally impossible, for I could never afford it.

Terri didn't make it until the following spring. She died before the end of the winter just like Angie and to this day is sorely missed by those who knew her. I went to see her in the hospice on the day she died, and said a painful goodbye, for she was unconscious by then.

Years before I had written the story of the

Archangels – 4 Great Forces of Light that are believed to surround the earth in protection of humanity. Initially I had written it for Sandy, and later made it into picture format for Ian. It became so popular with the groups that I had been asked to put it onto tape. When Terri fell ill, I promised I would finish it especially for her, and had recently done so, but was deeply disappointed that she wouldn't be able hear it after all.

As I left a hospice, I knew she was going to die during the evening, and prayed I would realise when she went. I felt unsure about my awareness, because I was teaching a large class in Southampton that night. For some reason, I took the Archangel tape along with me, and we lit candles for Terri all along the tables in the room.

I needn't have worried, for suddenly In the midst of class the electricity abruptly cut off, and I knew she was going.

Enshrouded in candlelight, I clicked on the tape, and 24 people in the class followed the meditation. They all felt they had linked with Terri, even though some didn't know her at all. As soon as the tape finished, the lights returned.

There was much discussion afterwards on how this could have possibly happened, for we all knew that the electric meter and light switches were nowhere near anyone in the room, and we were the only people in the building that night. For me, I saw no reason to doubt that my request had been granted. When I checked later, I was told that Terri had died at the same moment the lights switched off.

Shortly after the funeral, Terri's husband phoned, and offered the house to me again. He said it was her fervent wish that I should move there, and he was prepared to wait until I could afford it. He offered me a very good deal.

At first I couldn't see a way past the difficulties, but then suddenly everything started to happen. Someone managed to get a mortgage; someone else lent the money for the deposit, and my solicitor - whom John and I had known for a while – offered his services for free. When I saw him, all he asked for was the money I had in my pocket.

And so it was, that for just £3.10p, I moved into Worsley Street in the spring of 1986 - Terri's magic home of her dreams - a tiny two up and two down terraced cottage, with carpets and everything else necessary to completely furnish a house.

With a full and grateful heart I watched the trees slowly come alive with blossom and leaf, and admired the yellow beauty of a host of daffodils, carefully planted along the edge of the garden – a golden tribute to Terri's memory. Quietly, I stared out the window, sending my love and thanks to her, and remembered....

With almost no effort at all, I was now standing amidst this wonderful gift so generously given – and if that was not a message in answer to my request, then I was at a complete loss to know what was.

25 THE SINS OF THE FATHERS

It was only a year later when my father also died. He had a heart attack shortly before his 78th birthday on a chilly day in April 1987, and for me it wasn't really unexpected. After Terri's death, I began searching horoscopes to see if it was possible to determine "exit points", and thought I had found one in his.

Having such a strong feeling about it, I had warned both my brothers, and even hinted as much to Dad, as I was concerned for my mother and how she would cope without him. He wasn't frightened of dying, and I think he knew anyway, because afterwards I found his chart and other things I had sent him, neatly laid out in the upstairs bedroom.

The following circumstances were extremely traumatic, and in many ways seemed to drive the shaky foundations of our family further apart, for there was much I couldn't tell my brothers then. Dad had been drinking heavily at the end, and by the time he died Mum appeared to be permanently living in a deeply fragile state.

Keith, who lived locally, bore witness to some of the verbal attacks that often occur with drink, and I don't think that he could easily forgive Dad for the way he had behaved towards Mum during that time. Nevertheless, my father had suffered without any complaint for many years throughout my mother's illness, as well as developing severe Arthritis, as he got older. The combination must have been intolerable for him, so - even though his loss of empathy was not altogether excusable – I understood that maybe drinking was his only respite as the latter years closed in.

My finances were still dire, and there was no car, so I had to take the long journey home by train. I remember waiting on the platform, staring aimlessly at a large round metal clock, and thinking how insensitive and unremitting 'Time' was, as it ponderously ticked on by.

When I eventually got to my parents house, my father had been taken away. My brothers advised me not to go to the mortuary to see him. Mum was obviously in a very confused state, so it seemed unwise to leave her, but I did regret it afterwards.

It was decided that I should stay for a while, at least until after the funeral, and we tried to ensure the next few hours would pass as calmly as possible. However, that first afternoon, with everyone there, was really bad. Mum seemed over explosive in temper, and very angry with us in particular, so I suspect my brothers were glad to go home. She was never an easy person, and had the profound ability to accuse and attack at the best of times, so it was probably better for just one of us to try to cope with her alone.

There was a blustery wind that night, and I could hear my mother wandering around, repeatedly opening and shutting windows in the nocturnal hours. Bearing in mind the unpredictable behaviour of the day, I didn't go out to her. It used to make her very angry if anyone tried to interfere.

It was about 7 o'clock the next morning when I was woken by her calling urgently outside the bedroom door.

"*Geoffrey!* **Geoffrey!** Where are you?" Bleary with sleep, I came out the room to find her leaning over the landing balustrade, peering down the stairs.

"He's not there, Mum," I said quietly, placing a dressing gown round her shoulders, for she was only wearing a flimsy nightdress. She discarded it onto the floor.

"*Why?* Where's he gone?"

"He... *he died Mum.* Don't you remember?" She stared at me with frozen eyes before turning back into her bedroom and drawing the curtains with a rough tug. I followed her rather lamely. She ignored me and began making the bed, carefully pulling and wrapping the sheets as she had learnt as a nurse - tucking them in tightly, and fiercely pumping the pillows.

"Are you alright?"

"*No! Why would you think I'd be all right?* I'm going to the shops. Are you coming?"

She wandered off into the bathroom, shutting the door firmly behind her. Later, I walked to the high street with her, but she remained stubbornly incommunicative, dark and resentful in her own secret world. The day seemed very long, and once again turned into a somewhat changeable and precarious night, but nothing more was said about my father.

However, the next morning, the same thing happened – and it happened again the day after that. I really sympathised that she was in such deep distress, and appreciated her memory was always uncertain, but her indignant and erratic behaviour made the strain extremely difficult to handle.

It was so hard to have to repeatedly tell her about Dad, over and over again, when it just meant she would behave almost as if she didn't care. It wasn't easy to remain composed, but I had learnt long ago that getting emotional never worked.

The fourth day, I waited until I heard her go out onto the landing, and followed hurriedly, bracing myself for the same. She was fully clothed, and leaning over the banisters staring down as before. I started to say something, but she held up her hand to silence me.

"The baby's crying!" she announced in a hoarse whisper. Puzzled, I stopped, and listened,

"What baby, Mum? I can't hear anything"

"It's *always* crying, and I can't make it stop. It just keeps *on* and *on*."

I tried again, wondering if it was a neighbour's baby, but still couldn't hear anything.

"There's nothing, Mum. There's no baby here."

"**Listen!** Listen! It *is* there! It's always there! It never stops!" she put her hands over her ears as if trying to shut out the noise.

I moved to comfort her, but was shrugged away. She stood bent and rigid, peering down the stairwell, her head cocked to the side in intense listening mode, before turning sharply and walking down the red patterned carpet and into the lounge below.

I waited for a moment, still listening, before following her into the room. My mother was perched on the edge of her chair by the fireplace, fumbling to light one of the innumerable cigarettes she always smoked. She jumped nervously as I came in and dropped the matchbox, scattering its' contents over the green carpet. I noticed that most of them had been used, and she didn't bother to pick them up. I gathered things together, threw the dead ones in the bin, and carefully struck the remaining one for her, watching the smoke spiral, before saying,

"It's okay, Mum. It will be all right. It's a terrible time for you at the moment. You must be missing Dad very much."

She never usually inhaled, but this time she did, breathing in deeply as she remained staring into the room, before remarking in a low voice.

"I killed him, you know … I killed your father, didn't I?"

"No you didn't Mum."

"I did. And I killed his father… Geoffrey blamed me, and said I would kill him in the end too" She sounded quite resigned to the fact.

"You didn't kill them Mum – they both died of a heart attack."

"I did … I seem to kill everything." She broke off, brushing a stray bit of ash off the coffee table, before adding as if an after thought. "…. I killed the baby too."

"The baby? What *is* this about the baby?"

"Mother's baby. I killed it" Her voice was coldly matter of fact. "It kept crying, you see, and it wouldn't stop"

"What? …"

Horrified, I sank heavily onto the settee, feeling I had been punched in the stomach. Did she know what she was saying? She was always so confused, but she had repeatedly mentioned "The Baby" in the past. Something must be relevant there? I was aware I needed to try to remain composed and keep my voice low.

"Tell me, Mum… tell me… What are you trying to say?"

"I know *exactly* what I am saying!" she swung round in irritation, before announcing accusingly "You've pestered, and pestered me to tell you what happened, so now I *am* telling you!"

"But why today?"

"Because I realised they are all gone now, and I can say exactly what I want ... The baby was crying and crying ... I didn't know what to do, and nobody came to help ... "

My heart was racing, fearful of what she would reveal next, but she just remained there looking into space. I waited, feeling profoundly sick for I had begun to conjure up appalling visions in my head.

"Mum?" I asked gently, trying to get her to look at me. "*Mum?* ... Is this true?"

She didn't reply at first, and I peered at her closely, but she turned and gazed back with unwavering eyes, challenging me to disbelieve her. Finally she retorted,

"Whatever you all might think, I don't lie!" Her hands fidgeted shakily as she stubbed out the cigarette before continuing.

"Your father didn't believe me about the baby, because *my* father insisted I had imagined it. They didn't want anyone in the family to know... and your father didn't want me saying these things, and upsetting you children..." she trailed off.

They? I wondered randomly who 'They' were. Was this the truth? Or did she imagine it? I suddenly realised that I was actually terrified that it *was* the truth.

My mother continued to sit hunched on the edge of the chair, staring in front of her; rocking slowly to and fro whilst grappling with her memories. Eventually she whispered - as if to a confidant.

"You see ... the trouble is I can't cry. It won't come, and I don't know how to bear it. I can't bear the pain, you see – it won't stop ..."

Those small, desperate murmurs of anguish were to haunt me for many years to come. They hung mutely in the atmosphere: ghostly images of despair, mingling darkly with the tendrils of smoke and chill in the air.

I waited again, stricken and immobilised by such deep sorrow, continuing to stare at her blankly, but she didn't notice. The early morning sun peered through the leaded glass windows, placing strange triangular shapes across the walls, and it seemed like a long unearthly moment before she spoke again.

"I was only ten years old when mother died, and the baby was only just born. What was I supposed to do?" she paused, glancing at me briefly, before adding resolutely "And *you* didn't help. You just sat at the window and cried!"

"… But I wasn't …"

"I *told* you mother was dead!" Her voice rose in frustration. "She wasn't coming back, so why did you keep on waiting for her? She *knew* she would die, and begged me not to let her go. They killed her!"

"Who?" I queried, suddenly finding my voice as I remembered our conversation some while ago. "Did the Doctors kill her? How Mum? How did they kill her?"

"Doctors make mistakes and people die. I found out she was wrongly diagnosed when I became a nurse. I vowed I would find out the day mother died. Anyway, it was Father and that Doris who really killed her…" She was rambling now, and turned towards me angrily.

"The baby was crying and you didn't care! You didn't help. You just sat looking out the window and calling for mother, while I had to do everything when Amah ran away."

"Amah?"

*"**Our nanny!**"* She shouted, really irritated now *"Don't you remember?* We brought her from India to look after us all, but she ran away. She said mother's ghost tapped on the window in the middle of the night. You **must** remember!" My mother scowled fiercely, before adding,

"I banged and banged on the door, but Father wouldn't come out. He shut himself away. He just disappeared and shouted he mustn't be disturbed. We were all alone. *Why didn't you help?"*

"I ... wasn't there, Mum."

"There was snow everywhere. It was so cold. You could have helped!"

"I think you're confusing me with Joan" I argued quietly. "I'm not your sister, Mum. I wasn't there. I'm your daughter. You are talking to me, not Joan."

She stared at me then, her face locked for a moment in utter confusion, before replying crossly,

"Yes, I know!"

With that, she sank slowly back into the chair, and I knew the spell was broken. Picking up the cigarettes, she mechanically pulled one out of the packet before searching for a match. There were none left, so she carefully placed it back in the packet before wearily shrugging her shoulders.

"When do you want lunch?"

"Not now, Mum! We need to talk ..." but she was up and hurriedly tidying the cushions before heading for the door.

26 THE ULTIMATE BETRAYAL

A full half hour passed before I followed my mother into the kitchen, for I was still stunned by her sudden confession: both confused and desperately upset. Her abrupt disappearance from the room seemed quite overwhelming, as there was no way of knowing whether her story was actually true, and I really dreaded what it would mean if it was.

After a lifetime of medication she was definitely senile these days, and existed alone in the dark shadows of her subconscious. She was so emotionally charged; deeply suspicious, unforgiving, and extremely volatile a lot of the time, but I simply couldn't believe that this account was just a delusion, when it seemed so vivid in description.

It was really upsetting that she had broken off like that, returning to her usual unpredictable self as if nothing had happened. I feared I would never find out the rest of the story. However, it was indeed fortunate that the previous outburst had clearly opened a forbidden door, for she chose to continue that same afternoon.

After we had spoken, some of the anger seemed to have left her, and I found her happily chopping vegetables in the familiar old kitchen of my childhood. In a way it was comforting that it still housed the squat steel grey boiler, deep side dresser, and the same flat fronted blue and lemon units honed in the style of the 50s. The white butler sink had long since gone, but the square red tiles on the floor remained, and an old fashioned cooker stood in the corner.

It seemed important that we ate together, and as Mum was impatient to do this, we actually sat down to lunch at the long carved table in the dining room, as early as 11 o'clock that day.

We didn't speak while we were eating, and afterwards sat looking through the French Doors onto the garden. The budding 'Virginia Creeper' had already begun to spread its tentacles, ready to overtake the summerhouse as it did each year. Every autumn its canopy of red and gold always filled my mother with pride.

We remained silent, and I was wondering how we were going to pass the time in the afternoon, when she suddenly decided to talk to me again. She seemed remarkably lucid, reiterating the story with the familiarity of a newly found friend.

From what she said, I gathered that my grandfather was working on a secret invention, and needed to be in his own laboratory in Aberdeen. It was not long before Christmas and he decided to bring my grandmother back from India with him, for she was pregnant yet again and the baby was due in a matter of weeks. Amah – the Indian name for a nanny – came too, in order to look after my mother and Joan.

Unfortunately grandmother became ill with severe headaches and stomach pains, so the local doctor was called. Not realising that she had acute toxaemia he wasn't too disturbed by her condition, but advised her as a precaution, to stay in bed until the time of the birth.

My grandfather hired a young nurse to look after her. Someone he had met on his last visit to Scotland, but this was not a good idea, for the Italian blood of a heavily pregnant woman immediately took a profound dislike to her. Nevertheless, in spite of her pleading, the nurse stayed.

Three weeks passed with some upset I gather, as my grandmother was forced to stay trapped and alone in her bedroom for some considerable time, brooding over the failure of grandfather to come out of his laboratory, or bother with her at all.

The baby was eventually born prematurely a few days before Christmas under very difficult circumstances, for 1927 was the worse winter for many years. The house was so far from town that the family became completely snowed in, and there was no medical help.

After the birth, my grandmother fell even more ill and was quite incapable of looking after the baby. It seems that she became further distressed from being continuously alone, and one night went in search of my grandfather. It was a pitiful moment for her - and indeed for the rest of the family, for she eventually found him– fast asleep, with the nurse in his arms.

Mum didn't really know what actually happened then, but hysterical shouting woke her up, and she found Joan crying at the top of the stairs. There were shards of glass smashed in the hall, and she saw blood on the carpet, but the children were hurriedly removed back to bed.

"The next day Amah told us about it." Mum continued, lighting yet another cigarette as she talked. "She said something bad had happened. Mother had run out into the snow and got lost in the blizzard. People finally brought her back, but the snow was so thick it was lying in drifts everywhere. She looked a dreadful blue colour, and kept trying to hold my hand and say something, but she couldn't breath, and then collapsed with a terrible seizure. Joan was screaming, and father made Amah take us away."

"But I remember you said she didn't die then?"

"No. Later that day, the same people came again on snowploughs to get her, and I ran down the stairs because she kept calling me. Father tried to stop her, but she grabbed hold of my dress, and begged me to help her, and not let Doris go away with her."

"Doris?"

"Yes, *Doris!*" My mother sounded frustrated "*She* was the nurse!"

Noticing my confusion, she heaved a low sigh, speaking to me as if to a child.

"You must have realised the nurse was Doris?"

"No I didn't!" I was really surprised.

"Well she was! "She was impatient to continue. "Anyway, they took mother, but she didn't stand a chance and died on the way to hospital. Father locked himself in his laboratory, and soon afterwards, Amah ran away in fright She was certain she had seen mother's ghost tapping on the window... I don't know what became of her."

"And so you and Joan and the baby were left alone?"

"Yes" she replied, flatly. "I kept hammering on the door, but father just wouldn't come out, and I was really frightened. I didn't know how to look after the baby - it was so very tiny and looked so ill. I knew it had bottles, but mother's milk wasn't there anymore so I gave it our milk, except I didn't know I had to boil everything. It got big blisters in its mouth, and then eventually one night, it wasn't crying anymore, and when I went to get it ... it was very cold..." Her voice broke into a whimper.

"Oh dear God, Mum."

"I don't remember when Father did come out, but it was after the baby died ... I wrapped it in a blanket and was going to bury it when the snow melted. He was so very cross, and said I had killed it ... "

"How **could** he have said that?" I was absolutely furious.

209

"Well he *did* say it, and I don't think he ever forgave me, but then I never forgave him for doing what he did, or for marrying that woman so soon after mother's death."

We remained silent for a while - she with her memories, and me sickened by it all - wondering how she had been allowed to go through so much pain over the years. How could this have happened to such a young child, abandoned by everyone who should have cared for her and her sister. I looked up to find her staring at me.

"I suppose you don't believe me either," She said as a statement. "Nobody ever does."

"Yes I do" I didn't hesitate in reply. "I just wish I had known all this before."

"Father said we had to keep it a secret, so everyone said I was deluded … they tell me I'm mistaken, you see. It is best to keep these things secret anyway, because doctors don't understand and just prescribe more pills and injections. Besides, it would have caused big trouble in the family. Joan remembers, but she's a coward and wouldn't tell because she didn't dare disobey father."

"But she might tell now" I thought to myself quietly, amazed how lucid my mother still sounded.

"Tell me, Mum" I hesitated. "Why do you always call it The Baby?"

"Because that's what Amah used to say. Mother was so sick and nobody named it anything else. Joan kept saying it was Mary, but she had a doll called that. Anyway it was a boy, so I don't know why … and father was shut away and didn't care, did he?"

She got up suddenly, as if frustrated and bored with

the subject.

"Have you eaten?"

"Yes Mum! We have just eaten together! "She ignored my answer.

"I must feed the birds. There's some cake in the tin if you're hungry."

I followed her despondently into the kitchen, and watched her going down the path in the garden. My father always loved the birds, and she was obviously carrying on the tradition of leaving old remnants of bread soaked in milk out on the lawn. I hoped that maybe she was doing it for him.

She had clearly returned to her usual vague self, behaving as if nothing had happened, and I found this deeply saddening, especially as our discussion had been so traumatic. I wondered whether it was all those drugs that kept affecting her changeability, or, having been able to say her piece, had she chosen to forget what we had spoken about?

She looked an old, old woman now, my poor mother, who for so long had been forbidden to speak of her lost childhood. How really terrible that was, and it seemed all the more poignant as I watched her pottering aimlessly around that afternoon.

When it came to evening I went to bed early as I was totally exhausted, but of course I couldn't sleep. I could hear Mum wandering around opening and closing windows for what seemed like forever, until eventually all went quiet.

Relieved, I tiptoed down to the kitchen to fetch a drink, but could hear muffled noises coming from the lounge. Opening the door, I saw my mother sitting in the dark, her face strangely illuminated with shadowy light from the silent television and one small fire glowing in the room. She was smoking again, and knitting furiously, letting the cigarette droop from the corner of her mouth as she often did when concentrating.

"I thought you'd gone!" She seemed astonished.

"No, of course not. I was just getting a drink."

"Well, when you do go, make sure the curtains and windows are closed. We don't want the natives peering in."

At the time I had no idea what she meant, but later discovered that she was referring to the natives in India, where she had obviously returned in her mind.

"I will." I said quietly. "Good night, Mum." Carefully closing the door, I crept upstairs.

So there I was, sitting on the same bed that I had lain in so heartbroken, after they had taken my mother away many years before. I looked around the room and remembered - the same furniture, the same carpet, and ironically the light on the bedside table carried the same lampshade … but I was no longer the same.

The room was cold, yet I stayed there staring into my thoughts for a long time, struggling to make sense of the events of the day. The overshadowing of my dear father's death, my mother's heart breaking revelation – the fact that the baby was referred to as an "it", and never a sibling, a brother, or even a boy. Yes, so many changes had happened in such a short while, and I wondered vaguely if a karmic cycle had finally returned for us all - as a form of retribution?

My mother was so fragile, cranky, impossible to live with, and severely overrun by the hazards of life. She dwelt in this strange forbidding arena, unfamiliar to many of us; doing the most crazy of things, and often forgetting that she had thrown her false teeth away in the bin, but when she smiled, she was to me, the most beautiful person on earth.

I understood so much now about her behaviour over the years. Perhaps she was only reflecting or even hiding from the misdeeds in her past. What could be worse than the experience she had been forced to live through? How selfish of her father to insist it was kept a secret, and how wrong of my father not to allow her to speak about it either.

It seemed like this story belonged to somebody else: as if I was standing outside myself, observing events from far away. There was no emotion, yet bizarrely a tear formed and stayed there, cold on my cheek.

27 THE AFTERMATH

Mum and I didn't talk about anything much after that day, although she definitely seemed to be in a better frame of mind. She remained her usual erratic self and spent much of the time in shadowy silence. I was pleased, as I didn't want to talk anyway, and hoped that the conversation had helped her to feel more peaceful for a while. After all, if she couldn't find some solace and consolation for the past, whatever did she have left?

I wasn't too aware of what immediately followed. Events got jumbled up together. Those were very difficult days for we were all in much turmoil, and I was so undecided what to say to my brothers, if anything at all.

Simon came for the funeral and I was glad he was there, for his wise, gentle nature relieved the burden somehow. My poor mother didn't recognise him at all, and confided in me secretly that there was a strange man in the kitchen, making her a cup of tea!

The cremation came and went, and it was all much of a blur, except I sang in an over loud voice, which made Keith stare at me once or twice. Few people were there besides the family.

My father didn't believe in pomp and ceremony at funerals - or anywhere else for that matter. He didn't want flowers, for he said they would whither and die, which he considered quite ludicrous at a funeral. So, adhering to his wishes only one wreath was produced - a yellow one I remember. A man came along afterwards and held it up with aplomb, which made it seem even more starkly alone.

You see Dad was a free man inside, yet sadly he was never really free in life. We knew that he wanted to be cremated and his ashes scattered, but even that was not to be as he chose, for the wreath and subsequent burial of his ashes seemed so important for Mum.

Joan was there, but I only had one chance to talk to her very briefly. I asked about the baby and the infant death. She reacted very quickly, and with some upset, querying if I meant Mary. That was definitely some confirmation I suppose. I really wanted to talk to her, but just then my mother came up behind us, and, not wanting to upset the applecart on my father's funeral day, I didn't try to continue.

Mum made it completely obvious that she had very little time for Joan. They barely spoke, and didn't seem at all easy in each other's company. I decided to write to my aunt later.

Keith and I went to visit Dale at home sometime around then. Again I recall little of the meeting, except that Dale was very upset for he was so close to Dad that it obviously must have been a great loss to him. I do recollect that Viv was cross with me. She said that I had been no help to Dale over the years, for he had suffered dreadfully with it all, and I had just swanned in and out whenever it suited me. She was right of course, because, if you remember, that's what I had decided to do - everything else being so inexplicable to the family at the time? But in retrospect I suppose that was a wrong decision.

Sometimes I wonder if I had been more of a "normal" daughter – the sort that behaved in the correct domestic way - it would've been better for everyone. Viv certainly believed in family. She was a wonderful mother, and brought up three beautiful children. Everything was orientated in that direction and such a bonus for Dale. But things were so different in our household as we grew up. Generally we had always been in a rather contradictory and fragile state, which must have been difficult for others to understand, and on that day there did seem to be significant issues between my brothers about the rights and wrongs of the past.

Dale had certainly been greatly affected by his treatment as a child, and therefore had much sympathy for our father's continued difficulties. However, Keith definitely felt that Dad was very controlling, and wasn't altogether sympathetic to Mum's emotional needs, especially in later life. As usual, I was sitting with one foot in either camp - for irritatingly I could see both sides of the argument, and from where I stood, both were true. Anyway, there weren't any solutions. What was done was done, and already in the past.

Nevertheless, I realised very clearly that I wouldn't be able to tell Mum's story to either of my brothers until later. It was all too soon after the loss of Dad. After all I had waited long enough to hear the tale, so I suppose it wouldn't matter to wait just a little bit longer to repeat it.

I really wanted to tell them then though, for it explained so much. Dale was not unlike my grandfather in both looks and high intelligence, and Mum may well have seen in him a reflection of her father - or even herself, for she was the oldest offspring at the time of her mother's death. Being the second child and having the same birthday, she often mistook me for her sister Joan. Keith was the third child, and I could now see why he was looked after so gently and carefully, especially when he was a baby, for under the confusion of circumstance, maybe his birth had aroused the tragic echo of her long dead sibling?

The reasons for her behaviour towards us became glaringly obvious to me, and it made so much sense - not only why she had treated us all differently as we grew up, but also why she always found Christmas so difficult - so much so that she even died a week before Christmas. We youngsters must have subconsciously reawakened memories of her own terrible childhood, which perhaps she tried - and continued to try through her grandchildren - so very hard to resolve.

After the funeral Dad's ashes came home in a cheap brown plastic container. For some reason I found this terribly disrespectful and upsetting. It was made worse by Mum reacting really badly as well. She caught sight of me unexpectedly as I tried to take it upstairs, and went into such dramatic overload that I knew that I could never allow him to be buried that way.

I told her that we were going to use something else, but there was no reasoning with her for she was adamant that she didn't want such a 'thing' in the house, and remained greatly distressed. So, in a moment of quiet, I quickly hid it, and, when she next remembered, I told her that I had sent it back to the funeral directors. She didn't believe me, of course, and kept going in search of it, which was really worrying as it was quite possible she might find it, and throw it away.

If you know about mentally disturbed people, you will understand how astute they can be at times. My mother was suddenly resolutely 'there' just when I thought she wasn't concentrating. Trying to avoid continued upset, I began looking for another container in the middle of the night. I searched everywhere as quietly as possible, but she inevitably found me scrabbling around in the bottom of an unused cupboard, surrounded by rusty cake tins, whilst assuring her that I was just looking for something to eat!

So in the end, I felt there was no alternative but to empty out Dad's ashes into a very ordinary carrier bag - something she hopefully wouldn't notice if she happened to see it by accident.

I know this sounds absolutely horrific, but to me it was the only way forward. I wanted to be able to get out of the house without Mum, in order to find something to resolve the issue, but she was now being particular observant of my actions. So I decided to call my brother with some casual excuse, and I hoped that going out with such an unassuming item wouldn't cause undue attention.

The next day he dutifully appeared, and hurrying outside, I put the offending bag in the back of his car, feeling pleased there were other bits and pieces there, which made the appearance less obvious.

Keith and I spent absolutely ages searching for something that could be classified as suitable for Dad's ashes, but without any luck. We didn't go back to the funeral directors, because I think anything from them would have been too obvious and completely outcast by Mum.

Anyway the nearest we could get was a white casserole dish - dreadful, I know! However, it seemed to be something that Mum might accept, and by then we were really more than tired. On our travels we came across a huge whiskey bottle and half considered using that, but it was obviously out of the question. The idea broke the intensity for a moment through, for we both knew that Dad would have been highly amused.

It had been arranged for his ashes to be buried beside his parent's resting place, and Keith suggested it would be a good idea to try and tidy things up at the cemetery as well, so we went down to the dear old church in Footscray to prepare the place of my grandparents for Dad's arrival the next day.

When my grandfather died, my sweet grandmother wanted something living to be planted in his memory, and chose a beautiful bush of abundant red roses. Later, her ashes were also scattered there.

When we arrived, we could see the bush was still

alive and had completely enshrouded the grave. A small place had been prepared for Dad, and we cleaned things up as best we could, but it was sad, because everything looked so wild and unkempt.

As we were going, my brother saw a tidy bin at the side of the church. It wasn't very big, but he decided that as he had a few bits of rubbish in the back of the car, he would also get rid of them there.

However, to my horror he picked up the carrier bag that held Dad's ashes, and proceeded to try to dump it along with everything else! In great alarm I leapt to grab hold of it, and together we began a rather incongruous jig as I tried to pull it out of his hands.

For a long moment we jerked to and fro in stupefied silence, with Keith frowning weirdly at me as if I had suddenly gone mad.

"What *are* you doing?" he exploded, still grimly clinging on.

"Dad's in there!" I hissed, clutching wildly with one arm, whilst trying to envelop the complete bag in the other. It was lucky I did, as he immediately dropped it like a stone.

You know, it is terribly strange what people commit to memory, and what the subconscious chooses to forget, because Keith now says he doesn't remember much of that event. For me, however, the whole scenario from brown plastic "thing" to cake tins, to carrier bag, to casserole dish, will remain forever rooted in my mind.

At home Keith distracted Mum for a moment and I crept upstairs to hide both Dad's ashes and the dish in the large dark wooden drawers of a huge chest that dominated the old bedroom of my brothers. Looking around, I could see that everything had remained much the same in that room as well – two single beds with a square wooden table between them: a carpet that never fitted, and the familiar old lino emerging from beneath. How strange it all was - so much the same, but life so different.

Early that evening, after Mum had sat down to knit and watch the inevitable television, I decided that this would be the best time to make the necessary transfer, and seal the dish ready for the inauguration the next day.

I felt really bad that my father's wish to have his remains scattered wasn't going to happen. It seemed immensely unfair, and, after much angst, I decided the least I could do was to allow him to be partially free.

So, whilst transferring the ashes, I opened the bedroom window and carefully threw a few handfuls out to scatter amongst the early spring flowers at the edge of the lawn. The evening breeze caught them, tossing them in the air as they fell, and I whispered my apology into the wind, sending him all my love and hope for real freedom in his exciting new world.

The next day we buried Dad at the edge of the grave of his parents. The vicar raised an eyebrow when he saw the dish, but Mum didn't appear deterred at all. She just stared straight ahead as if nothing particular was happening; yet I hoped that inside she was more aware.

That evening we watched television together, and spoke very little. Later I went to draw the heavy pink patterned curtains around the bow window, and looked out on the road. The street lamps were alight, and we could hear a car repeatedly trying to start its' engine across the way.

My mother glanced up from her knitting, and looked at me ruefully.

"Do you think I will be able to learn to drive now?" she asked.

28 THE RAINBOW CHILDREN

Almost immediately after returning home, Ian and myself were on our way to Russia. We were travelling with Paul, a musician friend of Ian's, and seven youngsters, ranging in age from 5 – 12 years, with varying nationality, race and backgrounds. They were called "The Rainbow Children", and we were on a mission of peace.

Looking back over the last months before my father died, it was evident that I had undergone a great change of attitude since the autumn of 1986. During that time, rainbows had been appearing in every direction for some while, and this seemed a strong portent for the future, especially as the arc of seven colours had long since been recognised as a bridge between the Creator and our world.

During that time, I can't say I was riding high, but did feel that at last we were going somewhere.

October 11, 1986 was the date of the nuclear disarmament summit between Russia and America in Iceland - an historic event of unity, later to be sealed by Gorbachev and Reagan as representatives of their respective countries.

Always with an eye on publicity, Ian arranged for us to go to Washington on the day of the summit. The children had already been brought together and given the Rainbow name, and we knew that many people appreciated the importance of allowing the next generation to express their opinions about the safety of their world. In fact I had already outlined a story about these children and their aims for peace.

Full of anticipation, we embarked on what seemed a huge project at the time, but for Ian nothing was impossible.

We arrived in America on a flash visit with a view to firstly stopping at New York, where the children would sing some of Lennon's more poignant songs in Central Park on October 9th - the anniversary of his birthday.

Having gone to the US with such wonder and excitement about this country of dreams, I cannot tell you how deeply affected I was, and looking back after the recent experience with my mother, it seemed even more distressing.

Right at the start, I didn't like New York. I found it very restrictive and threatening, despite the apparently expansive and open approach. I recollect thinking how contradictory it was, and feeling that if anyone else said that throw away line - "Have a nice day" - I certainly wouldn't!

On our way to our hotel in Manhattan, the taxi drove into Harlem. I saw people standing aimlessly in doorways, glaring at us as we passed on through the poverty of their time. There was hatred in their eyes; hatred for the systematic betrayal of their race, and I instinctively knew that, even if we could do something then to rectify the abuse of centuries, it was all too late - for here was a place where the soul of trust had died.

The hotel was modern, but black everywhere, teamed with a sort of musty yellow – bedding, paintwork, walls, and corridors – with bars on every window.

Paul, being a great musician, worked really hard to set up everything for the following day. He was one of those people who always had a smile on his face, and seemed to be enjoying the experience. Everyone, including the children, appeared totally awestruck and unaware of any atmosphere, so I had to accept that the problem was entirely mine. We all ate jumbo food in the small cafeteria, and finally went to bed. That night, I burned candles in my room, and in the morning they had turned black too.

The time in Central Park was actually quite moving, as Yoko overheard the music and invited us all up to the Dakota building for tea. We didn't stay long, but it was quite impressive. There were guards there, with vicious looking dogs, and the building smelt faintly of polished metal, but the apartment was spacious, comfortable and not in the least ostentatious. When we left, we were each given a signed poster that boldly stated "WAR IS OVER – If you want it", and, even at that time, I sadly wondered how many people really cared.

It was better in Washington – the air was purer, the way less crowded, and the buildings less ominous. Putting aside my disappointment, I chastised myself for, after the threatening presence of the long Cold War, this was indeed an event to remember. How innocent the children looked as they paraded outside the White House - the future generation, hopeful and unassuming amidst the bigger picture of history, as two mighty nations met at last in an attempt to walk together in peace.

Our presence didn't go unnoticed by the media, and so 6 months later here we were on the second lap of this strange adventure, packed tightly in a rickety Russian plane journeying to Moscow. The children were restless, and a man was snoring in my ear. Clutched on my lap, was an old teddy bear of mine, called Geoffrey. I said I had brought it for the children, but in retrospect, I guess it was more for me than them.

I remember very little about the timing of events. I don't know where we stayed, or what exactly happened, except the food was strange, and the atmosphere was far better than in the autumn before. This too was a really important event, for it was the first time that Russia peered out through a chink in the Iron Curtain, two years before the fall of the Berlin Wall, which heralded the end of communism.

The arrival of the Rainbow Children was shown on the news in both countries, whilst - symbolic of the unity between the two nations - they sang with a Russian child choir in Red Square. It was a proud moment for them and their families, and they were later to appear on the Wogan show, which was very popular at the time.

Feeling particularly emotional, I looked around the famous Red Square in awe; studying the beautiful domed buildings, with those spires of fire red glinting like mosaic in the sun. How mighty yet innocent it seemed, and on the surface not at all like my recent experience of Manhattan's overbearing edifices, bars on the windows, and dark unease in the streets between.

We visited the Kremlin and an antique bus proudly took us on a tour throughout the streets of Moscow packed full of ramshackle cars, hooting with intent whilst seemingly going every which way but forward. The buildings were dilapidated but we could still see the remnants of a decadent past – an exquisite memory of white structures and tall arches that held a silent pain of their own, reflected in the mirror of austerity behind closed doors.

Here was a country locked in the 1950s. There was a gentle, lonely, innocence about the people we met, which stood out in contrast to the United States. Although that young nation was perhaps not so innocent, it seemed to me that many of their people were equally lonely, and even overwhelmed by the pressures and affluent trappings of the "American dream".

So there we were, our personal joys and tragedies standing amidst the bigger picture of 'National Pride', and inevitably - whether the outcome be fortuitous or not – we would all have to find our own way through the decisions made by our leaders, and deal with what kind of future those decisions would personally hold for us.

In spite of the achievement, and reaction of the media, for some reason I didn't feel refreshed or hopeful about the future, but more than a little troubled and sad.

****

The saying "Give me a child until it's seven years old…." could not have been more apt in the days that followed, and for someone whose background was instilled with the urgency to always search for an explanation – either through reason or faith - this was indeed a precarious time.

Less than one week after the return from Russia, an icy hand reached out, wrapping around me as a dark nameless shape, and my heart felt as if it was being ripped from my body by the hurt of it all.

There seemed no logic or reason for the mood that suddenly overcame me, and no way I could explain anything, least of all the incident that passed between my mother and myself before my father's funeral. I realised then that, contrary to what I had hoped, it would be a long while before I would be able to describe what happened to my brothers.

Initially I did try to discuss this with Sandy, but even with her I couldn't bring myself to specify clearly what had happened.   Yet strangely it was as if she already knew - quite often adding detail I had forgotten to mention, or finishing sentences for me,

"You sound sometimes as if you were actually there," I said once.

"Well, I do think I *was* there, sometimes" she

replied, "It is almost as I am seeing everything just as it happened". She waved her hands in a questioning gesture, "It's a really weird feeling, and I don't think it is just a psychic impression. Everything is too clear."

We were both used to these sorts of impressions by now, and Sandy was much more accepting of her undoubted psychic talent. The reactions of both her and my mother ever since the first encounter did seem very strange. I shrugged inwardly, readily accepting the feeling. From what I had learned I wouldn't disbelieve anything these days.

I tried to get back into life, but the dreadful inner pain just wouldn't go away, preventing me from processing anything productive for days. I didn't think I was behaving any differently – just not functioning very well – but Ian didn't seem at all sympathetic. He told me later, he felt as if I had shut him out completely, and even John said I wasn't there with him anymore, but living in a silent world of my own. He had moved up north a few weeks before, but we still kept closely in touch. I missed him very much, but in retrospect it was probably essential that I had this time alone.

How deep is grief I wonder? Surely, for each individual it can never be the same? For me, it crept up like a silent assassin, waiting in the shadows to grip me with grey fingers when I was not aware.

It's so difficult to describe pain isn't it? It has so many faces, and all of them dark. If I could put into words how bad this was, I would, but I can't, and I suppose nobody can do that when it comes to self.

The worse thing was that I didn't even know it was grief at first, and when I did I just couldn't comprehend it. I was totally in tune with other worlds, and knew they existed without any doubt. I *knew* about death. It was a beautiful and sacred experience. I understood it. I *taught* people how to deal with it, and I had grieved

227

before, but this was almost more than I could possibly bear.

So I did the only thing I could do – I shut down emotionally – just as I had done as a child - and closed the door on my heart, with my thoughts.

29 THE HEART'S AGENDA

For the next long night I wandered aimlessly around the little terraced house that once belonged to Terri, unable to settle anywhere. I sat in the front room for a while gazing into the flames of the open gas fire, set into the wide brick chimney stack that separated the tiny lounge from the dinning room behind.

"So there we go," I thought. "An incident happens; a life passes, and one day we will all end up at the beginning again. For now, those of us left will continue to live our lives, but happiness disappears when grief arrives".

I was disgusted with my grandfather's selfishness, but also cross with Dad. He had died without any of us knowing the truth, because he had chosen to believe the word of in-laws over that of his wife.

Mum hadn't been allowed to release her anger and pain: to speak about how she felt: to lay the ghost of her mother, or the death of the baby. She had never been allowed to do that, so that anger and pain, came out on us – her children.

Why didn't he realise that? I wondered. But if he didn't believe it had ever happened, I suppose he could hardly anticipate it arising in the future.

Restlessly, I got up and moved through to the back room, sitting at the large pine table that overshadowed the area. There was little space for anything else. It was my teaching table – an ancient relic that enabled me to house eight to ten students at any given time. It all seemed hollow and empty right then. There were candles on the table and I lit them.

I wanted to cry, but I couldn't. I just sat there in the gloom amidst the flicker of flames; staring at the shadowy lunar shaped light that emanated onto the wall from the kitchen behind.

It was time for my father to move on, but I didn't realise how difficult it would be, or how bad the loss. I thought I knew all about these things, but how wrong I was. His strength had always been a powerful cornerstone for me, and for a brief moment in history, he had lived, and then he was gone.

"Was that really all that was left of his life?" I wondered. "Some socks in a drawer, a casserole dish, and ashes in a carrier bag? Was that really all that was left to say he was here?"

"There are always memories, dear, there are always memories."

I could hear the wisdom of my sweet grandmother in my ear, and I smiled sadly. At the moment the memories just didn't seem enough.

And what about my mother? She had been sorely betrayed, and frightened all her life. Yet, after our conversation, she had returned to her twilight world just as easily as she had left it, treating me as if nothing had ever been said. She was so used to hiding it I suppose. However, I knew that neither of us would ever be the same again. We had shared her terrible secret together, and I felt honoured that she had trusted me enough to reveal it. But what would happen to her now? It was quite impossible for anyone to live with her any more - least of all her children... least of all me...

I wandered into the kitchen to make a coffee, and stood there between the tightly packed units, peering out into the lean-to at the side of the house. The little window boxes on shelves were filled with spring flowers. The kettle spluttered into life, and I remembered that only a year before I was warm with gratitude for being allowed to live in this magical place, yet now so coldly immobilised with sorrow.

I made a coffee, but forgot to drink it, and sat down at the table again.

No, it wasn't *just* about that, was it? This distress was not only about the loss of my father, or my mother's pain, but also the loss of my sibling family. This terrible thing had torn our unit apart and, along with our children, we three had learned to live quite separately in our different worlds.

After the funeral, I had said goodbye to my brothers, and sadly realised that there was little to hold us together now Dad was gone. I wanted to be in touch with them both, but felt we were so distant from each other, and didn't even know if they would want to see me at all.

Rightly or wrongly I didn't think they would ever really understand the road I had followed in life. It just wasn't "normal". And if the truth was known, perhaps I was frightened of rejection, or being accused of behaving "hysterically" like Mum. Dad always used to worry about that with all of us. Siblings we were: we would always care, but maybe we would remain only strangers now. Somehow I knew it would be a long time before we would see each other again.

Eventually I got up; stiff from sitting, and slowly climbed the little spiral staircase, before crawling into bed. For a long while I lay there staring blankly, as the candle in its' domed container danced diamonds on the ceiling.

My mind refused to shut down, returning my thoughts to our recent excursion abroad. How small was our personal world and yet so vast in its importance against the so-called bigger picture of nations as they proudly strutted on the stage of life - viewing each other in distorted mirrors, as if at a funfair.

How insignificant were the parades, the stardom, the publicity, the fears and the wars – the repetitive horrific wars.   How tiny and irrelevant against the enormity of the universe, and I had to ask myself - was this actually the "real" world we were living in, or just a terrible caricature of what it was meant to be?

A cloud moved on past the window, allowing the crescent moon to shine silently through the open curtains.   A shaft of pale azure light found its' way across the room, and eventually its' gentle glow enabled me to fall into a fitful sleep.

I awoke at dawn, and, taking a chair, padded barefooted into the spare bedroom to watch the sun rise over the multi-patterned shrubs in the back patio. A neighbour's cat sprung over the fence, and slunk silently behind the bushes. It peered up at me guiltily as I opened the window, but didn't shift. I wondered if this one would move in like the others.   There was always one that wanted to stay, even though they continued to go home for their suppers.

Cats and birds seemed to be permanently around me, and Winston at the previous house even made friends with a blue-tit once. I found him in his favourite chair one morning, purring like an engine with the bird chirping happily on the arm beside him.

Then there were crows…there always seemed to be crows – either squawking on windowsills or tapping on windows, eyeing me darkly with looks askance. Three of them came and sat on the fence just before my father died, together with a loud-mouthed Siamese cat that appeared from nowhere and insisted on taking my pen away when I was trying to write in the garden. John was there at the time, and found it very amusing. He said it was a "portent", and bearing in mind the ensuing events, he was obviously right.   In my world I had learnt there was no such thing as co-incidence.   I smiled to myself as I remembered such times – cats and crows would certainly have got me burned at the stake in bygone years.

For a long while I continued to sit there, trying to focus. Terri had asked that I filled this little house with life and laughter, yet all I could do right now was to analyse everything through the eyes of death.

I had to find a way to stop thinking; trying to find answers; just for a little while, to allow for my heart to recover. The intellect is fine. There has to be reason and logic in life, but in the final analysis, the heart rules, and the heart is not reasonable or logical – it just is. So I had to make space for the heart – to give in, and accept that it has its own agenda.

Trying to relax, I looked around at the walls, glowing mutely in the light of the morning sunshine.

"There is nothing so mysterious and silent as an empty unused room", I said out loud, and it suddenly felt imperative that I brought it to life.

I had already started to decorate but had not got any further than building a unit that would house a comfortable single bed for any visitor who may want to stay. I had decided that, with a lid over it when not in use, it would also suffice very well as a large altar for candles and crystals. The soft cream on the walls emanated a certain peace that was important to cultivate if it was also to be a room for temple meditation.

Making a decision, I went to the unit, removed the lid, and pulled out copies of old Egyptian prints that I had been saving. I found paintbrushes, and black felt tip pens, leaving them in the room, before returning with a marmalade jar full of water, the kitchen radio, and a rickety old table that I kept in the garden.

Then, almost robotically I dressed in a well-worn tie-dye two-piece, and launched barefoot out to the shops on a mission to make life-size images of the prints, created by enlarged photocopies of various sections.

I bought small pots of paint in bright colours, accompanied by others of white, silver and gold; purchased enough food, wine and cigarettes to last for a few days, and finally, laden with my goods I returned home, for I knew what I was going to do – I was going to build an Egyptian Temple.

Switching the wireless to Radio 4, I began to decorate, paste and paint, staying there for hour after hour. The radio was on to stop me from brooding, but I perversely carried on thinking anyway. There were so many things to process. It was no good continuing to try to attract the media. However great the success, it would only be a nine day wonder, and end up on the back of a newspaper soaked in chip fat in somebody's bin.

I realised with a terrible intensity that what I had learned through all those years of study didn't mean anything at all … It couldn't really mean anything to anyone else until – as Stuart had so rightly said – it was brought down to earth, and used for a purpose. And what that meant was less pomp and ceremony, and much more realistic enchantment, cloaked in a simple language that could be understood by everyone if they chose to listen.

Yes…that's what I had to do. Try to help people to get to really know themselves – not be afraid to pluck their own star from the sky, and step by step bring it down to earth, where it could be used for a purpose. It was too late for my mother, but maybe in her name, it might help others?

"Everything does have its' purpose", I reasoned, and was unexpectedly grateful to America - for my shock and sadness about that unpredictable "dream" had unwittingly opened the door to allow me to release my grief. The deep pain of Harlem, and bewilderment over all the on-going, unseen torments of so many lives, including my own, were still there within, but soon I would be ready to begin again.

For four days I worked, and very rarely ate or slept, with the radio murmuring all the while. In the dark hours I continued to paint in the dim light, and when exhausted lay down on the single makeshift bed, surrounded by the flickering flames of miniature candles, dancing all around.

But I didn't think any more, because I became encased in the magic of creation. In the end, creative power overrides the thoughts, and seeing the splendour of construction coming alive on the walls, with the colours carefully edged in black, I became totally caught up in the moment.

On the fourth day I finished, wearily turning off the radio, and sitting down to survey the scene. The final outcome was far more beautiful in the candlelight than I had first envisaged, for the colours glittered with slivers of white and silver, and the golden treasures shimmered brightly amongst the static images.

As I quietly watched, a faint sound came into the room, and the atmosphere changed. I waited, listening intently and then, for the second time in my life, felt a hand, firm and comforting, on my shoulder. The feeling overwhelmed me, taking away the pain and filling me with peace in just the same way as happened before, all those years ago – but this time I knew who it was…

A gentle movement: a touch of breeze on my cheek, and my dearest father was gone.

I continued to sit there in silent sorrow, yet so very grateful for the experience. This was my family and my history; this was my past that had moulded the present, but I had learned much, and could make another new future, for the boys and myself, from the moment that was here.

Able to rest at last, I lay down for the last time on the faithful bed in the room. The sudden connection, and subsequent release had made my heart beat fast, and, putting my hands across my chest to ease the sensation, I lay there looking out at the stars, sending great love, and wishing my father well for the new life that would soon be his.

The light from the candles sparkled, illuminating the colourful Egyptian figures on the walls, as I quietly mused. Then slowly, as realisation eventually dawned, I began to laugh. Yes I had built a temple all right, but lying there in that position, I saw that in my grief I had also placed myself in an Egyptian tomb!

It had been a terrible time, but I knew it was over. My father was gone, my anger had melted, and it was time to move on, but I wouldn't forget, or let my mother down in the promise I had made her.

"One day I *will* tell your story, Mum", I whispered as I fell into a deep dreamless sleep. "…And when I do, people *will* believe you, I promise."

30 NEW LIFE AND LAUGHTER

*"Through the window yesterday I saw a fool talking to
himself, and it made me laugh, until I realized it was a
mirrored window."*
Jarod Kintz

I had always believed that everything has its'
purpose, but didn't appreciate how much death would
influence the direction of my destiny. The last
experience changed my life beyond everything
previously imagined.   It completely altered the way I
had focused my energy from that dramatic pledge of
childhood to the moment of confrontation at the
doorway of Spiritual understanding.

Nevertheless, all was not lost just because of past
events, or my failure to realistically help my mother.
Her life had become my life over the years, and this
had enabled me to look at the world in a way I may
never have done without that experience. The path I
followed had been my choice, and however obscure
the prospect of success, this was not the time to turn
back. I reasoned that sadly nothing could change what
had happened to her, but it was important that I should
now direct my energy in a way that may help others in
the future, and perhaps ensure that her suffering had
not been in vain.

During the following years, I threw everything into
developing a place where people could meet and
discover themselves: formulating courses, creating
meditations, and making them come alive by mingling
pieces of music together.   The workload was
tremendous, but I continued to be driven by a sense of
unending purpose, whilst gratefully gathering a wealth
of supporters along the way.

And from the moment I changed direction,
concentrating my attention on building a mystery

school, everything seemed to magically fall into place.

The little terraced house was first to become Master of Events, and as fast as I started one class, another followed in its' shadow, eager to take its' place.

But it was such a tiny house, with insufficient room to expand, so as others joined, and one course continued into another, enough space for everyone rapidly became of a premium.

Ian had put so much time, effort, and money into everything, but remained incredibly loyal: never complaining when I took another direction. It was entirely because of his continued support, I was eventually able to move to a much larger house in the centre of Southsea. For me, this place will always remain the most important and greatly loved dynasty of Maat, for it took a gigantic effort to bring it back to life after many years of neglect.

Campbell Road was a large Victorian building, topped by a formidable Dutch style gable. Set back from the road, with small gardens front and back, it housed ten rooms on 3 floors, with a sizeable basement below, and a magnificent larder extending into the hall, looking very like a Tardis from the outside. It was cheap, totally neglected, and left empty for over 5 years for it was said to be haunted: but I absolutely loved it from the beginning.

Most people found the idea of taking it on extremely daunting, but I was really excited by the prospect, even though the place was little short of derelict. Anyway, against advice from many, Ian found a way for me to move in, complete with nothing, in early January 1990.

Regretfully, I had to leave the little terraced house, but for some while afterwards it became a home for Matt and his wife Manda - along with Jemima, an inherited marmalade stray who was the latest feline tenant to have moved in.

My long suffering sons thought I was making a terrible mistake, for they didn't share my vision, and I believe poor Simon really felt weighed down with the responsibility of trying to talk some 'sense' into a mother who, to his mind, continuously made shambolic decisions.

Matt, being interested in the building trade by then, took one look at a carcass with a crumbling back, no carpets and giant holes in the walls, before advising me sincerely that it would be ridiculous to take this on by myself, as I would seriously regret it.

However, something told me that it was destined to work regardless of the enormity of the task, and I set about the project with one thing in mind – to try to pass on what I had learned to others: to show them we were all living in a massive school, and in charge of our own destiny: so if we didn't like the world we lived in, we could change it. Life wasn't about blame, success, or failure, but learning the art of living, right here and now, in our earthly kingdom.

I had no qualifications except that of experience, but along with enthusiastic conviction, this goes some way in persuading people that you may have something to say.

Gary – a long-standing student, and beautiful but very fragile soul - moved in too, and together we shared the desperate cold of the winter, for in the beginning the place was wide open to the elements at the back, and only shielded by a tarpaulin.

Ian organised a new wooden structure at the rear, and provided an old blue carpet from one of his county shows. It was incredibly thin, but so big it covered the large hall, stairs, landing, and even one room. So this was a perfect start.

People came from everywhere to help: filling up the wide hall with logs, ends of carpets, material to cover the walls, light bulbs, curtains, bits of furniture, and more. They scrubbed floors, cleaned windows, and washed kitchen towels: then wallpapered, painted, and stacked bricks that would hold planks of wood to provide shelves for the books.

A tramp left an unfortunate calling card in the porch, but I think we had taken over his domain, so perhaps he was a bit disgruntled.

One of the students donated an electric tea urn from their catering company, for we had no hot water at all and no way of heating it other than using a hairy looking plug socket in the kitchen.

And then there was Barry the builder – a medium associate of Tony, who gave a tremendous amount of expertise and physical effort. I had known him for years, and he really was the mainstay in the first steps of renovation.

Trevor, the traffic warden, came along with him to help, and in his enthusiasm accidentally dismantled a gas pipe in the basement. It wasn't until the following morning a huge leak was discovered. But we must have been remarkably well protected, because Gary and I both smoked, and the house had been filled with candles all through that night.

A horrified gas engineer was having the vapours with so many people around, whilst hoarsely shouting, *"Evacuate this building immediately!"* when some big mouthed people barged through the open front door, nosing everywhere and asking if the house was for sale. However, they didn't stay long, as Barry casually informed them we were about to blow it up.

There was no advertising, but would be scholars continued to appear. During that winter it was really surprising they stayed, for with only the odd Calor gas fire, every room was an icy reflection of the artic. They arrived wearing boots, balaclavas, huge coats, and fingerless gloves: sitting for 3 hours a session, enduring the elements with fortitude. Amongst them were Lorraine and Paul: two people that were to make a big impact in the future.

Lorraine introduced herself as a Gemini and was something of a sceptic in the early stages. I don't think she thought she would be with us long, as she only came out of casual interest in the beginning.

She was petit, lively, clever, and openly friendly, but didn't suffer fools lightly, and could pack a good verbal punch when passionate, which caused her a few problems along the way. However, with her intense sense of purpose, generous heart, and exceptional integrity, she remains one of the most genuine people I have ever met.

Paul was already an avid student before I moved, and became very special to me during that time. He was the musician that had been abroad with us: a wonderful, comforting person, with exceptional creative talent. The great thing about him was that he was highly intelligent and extremely emotionally aware. His smiling presence and good humour lit up the atmosphere, for he was fascinated by everything, and really interested in the lives of others.

Matt always said Paul looked like Ricky Gervais from 'The Office', and I guess he did really. He was 16 years younger than me, but the beauty of his music and boyish wonder endeared me to him, and I suppose that's why he was soon to fulfil the role of the musician my father had predicted.

We had a strange relationship really: based much more on friendship than emotional entanglement. Paul was a free spirit: like John: like me, and maybe that's why we have always got on so well. He had great respect for my feelings for John, especially when he died, and I will always be grateful for his empathy and sympathetic ear. The music he wrote for the Archangels as well as some of the temples was all encompassing, and because he had such a deep magical voice, we used it many times on the tapes. Being a natural teacher, it wasn't long before he joined Sandy and others taking classes.

Many people came just out of interest, but others had lived through unimaginable nightmares: suffering greatly from loss, poor health or appalling abuse. It was so rewarding to know that the sessions did perhaps offer a moment of respite: giving them a chance to believe in something, and maybe find a goal for themselves.

However, no one should go away with the idea that everything was doom and gloom, or we were attempting to "issue forth" as a barrel of saints. If the earth plane was a schoolroom, then surely the challenge was to learn to know who we really are, and laugh at our idiosyncrasies rather than take everything so seriously?

I reasoned that laughter was as much part of the Divine as any other aspect of life, and learning to use it in the face of fear was the key - for fear clearly has it's own mind, and its' power grows when feeding on itself. Through our attitude, we make our own heaven or hell, and part of the enjoyment is to allow ourselves to be ridiculous, even if it is unwitting at times.

So, if ever I became in danger of becoming too big for my cassock, I was rapidly shown that the world is not only a school and a stage, but also a platform for comedy, which I found to my cost with Paul one day.

Paul's talent for music was exceptional, and through trying to balance long periods of creation with various venues of work, his hours became very erratic.

So we established a studio for him in the basement, and fixed him up with a little chest of drawers inside a small wardrobe built for his gig clothes, and a single bed to use when he came home very late, but didn't want to disturb me. However in order to do that, we had to remove the inside stairs to the basement, and the only way of getting in there afterwards was down the outside steps in the garden.

This didn't really matter, as we made a hatch door in the floor of the Tardis upstairs - directly over the open top of the wardrobe - which we could lift to communicate to each other, and pass essentials up and down as needed.

One particularly exhausting day, Matt and Manda took Paul to the pub to relax. However, extreme tiredness left him very drunk, and Matt phoned to say that he had insisted on walking home alone, but kept tripping up kerbs and zigzagging erratically between the road, traffic, and various shops.

It was very late, but I decided to wait up to make sure he got back safely. Ages went by and I became more than a little worried, so I decided to see if he had got to the basement. Going down the steps in the freezing rain, I found the place locked, and was furious when nobody answered. Either he hadn't come home, or arrived there unannounced. For no particular reason I felt extremely insulted, and decided that the only thing to do, to find out if he was there, was to get into the basement via the trapdoor in the floor of the Tardis.

I returned upstairs, lifted the flap and lowered myself precariously down onto the little chest of drawers below. Unfortunately I hadn't secured the hatch properly and it slammed onto my head: the shock rapidly pushing me southwards, sending my feet straight through the fragile top of the chest of drawers with a resounding crack.

If you can imagine how it feels to find yourself shut in a wardrobe with a trap door on your head, a red shirt draped over one shoulder, and your feet confined in a very small space, you will realise how hard it is to keep your balance.

For a desperate moment I cavorted in the top drawer, before taking a giant step forward, and bursting out through the wardrobe doors, yelling in a mammoth voice,

"What the HELL's going on?"

Landing on a passing slug, whilst staggering onwards trying to hold myself upright, I caught a glimpse of Paul in the bed, sprawled on his back in the moonlight. Grunting, he raised his head vertically off the pillow and peered into the room, before slumping back again with a deep groan.

Suddenly the whole stupidity of the situation grabbed me, and I ran out of the flat, up the front steps, and back into the house, cackling inanely. It was a full hour, plus half a bottle of wine later, before I could stop laughing.

The next morning Paul sheepishly appeared, and slumped into a chair before requesting a cup of tea. He looked awfully white.

"Didn't you sleep well?" I asked, innocently.

"Not really" he said, "I had a dreadful nightmare, but it seemed so real at the time. I heard loud thumps coming from inside the wardrobe, and all of a sudden you swooped out, bellowing *'What the HELL's going wrong?'* in a terrible voice, before vanishing into the night, wailing like a Banshee."

When we recovered, we recycled the chest of drawers in the garden: filling it with juicy Hosta leaves – a memorial to the squashed slug.

31 THE WORLDS OF SELF

"I am not what happened to me, I am what I choose to become."
Carl Jung

As the years rolled on, I don't think I saw anything of my brothers, and had little contact with my mother, except by vague and rather baffling phone conversations. She asked me how my mother was once, and was utterly amazed to discover it was herself. She made it very clear she didn't want anyone to live with her, which rather left Keith to take over her care. Sadly though, she no longer saw him as the favoured son, mistaking him for Dad, and became very offensive at times. I did wonder that maybe the end result of our upbringing was for all of us, including her, to struggle on alone.

It was selfish of me not to appreciate Keith's difficulties, and although I did have my reasons, I regret not giving more active help during her latter days. Nevertheless, the pain of her life constantly stayed with me, and everything I subsequently attempted to achieve, was always with her in mind.

People continued to come from all walks of life, including both ends of the spectrum: the jobless to the affluent: teachers to college students: lawyers to housewives: even a few doctors, numerous nurses, social workers, and business associates. Some stayed for a little while, and some for many years, but they all wanted to know more – about themselves, the universe, and other worlds around them.

Although all different in nature, these were people of like mind: working together, discussing and exploring their hopes and fears, and learning from the past. Many formed friendships that have lasted to the present day

Each group chose a name, often after a constellation, and nobody seemed to mind when some of their peer groups secretly altered the title to a more fundamental equivalent. Hence Starweavers became known as "Cosmic Cobwebs": Emerald Grail as "Green Mug", and Great Bear as the "Big Yogi", to name but a few.

It was interesting that humour remained very much part of the sessions, but also that many of those who came were far from credulous – being full of intelligent and sceptical questions about what initially must have seemed rather far fetched ideas. Indeed, this gave me pleasure - having been the worst questioner myself.

Most were objective enough not to dismiss anything out of hand, and always remained open for discussion. All that was asked of them was not to accept everything as true, but to try out ideas: determine for themselves, and if they really wanted to discover, they would find their own proofs.

Jenny loved the early days, for she said she found the sense of discovery very exciting. And Sandy, with her infinite imagination, became a fantastic coach in those role model sessions of magical images, planets and signs.

In fact it really was great fun, both for them and myself. To watch people making their own discoveries and to see the sudden light of realisation dawning on their faces was one of my greatest joys. Teachers can only be guides to interpretation, and I knew that they had got there entirely through their own reasoning. After all, nothing is really original in thought, and maybe the job of a tutor is to just help others remember?

The subject of "Self" is really quite stimulating, for there are so many aspects to explore, and generally in life, we are not really encouraged to decipher more than those associated with the earth plane: often relying on others "more qualified" to even do that for us.

In my day it was considered "egotistical" to spend time on trying to find out "who we are", but things have changed now - although sometimes I feel that in this 21st century the pendulum has swung too far in the other direction over a number of ideas, and still often misses the point.

You see, we are made up of a jumble of things, from the physical body to spiritual desire: we are personalities, but we have a soul and spirit – maybe young, maybe old – and ancient teachings have always said that by getting to know who we really are, we can discover how to truly fulfil our purpose in this earthly life. People are designed for certain things, and everyone has their own personal function and role to fulfil in the Cosmic Plan.

But to get to understand how we "tick" is hard work; it doesn't come overnight, and we have to be committed to ourselves. I am not sure everyone found that part of it so enjoyable, for to "Know Self" is to challenge "Self" and take full responsibility for our feelings, thoughts and actions. It is fascinating and inspiring, but takes courage, for it requires continuous objective monitoring, and as I had previously discovered to my cost, most of us are unwitting masters of disguise, particularly to ourselves.

It is doubtlessly a struggle to find enough control to do something for the sheer joy of doing it, yet with no expectation of the end result: to take care we don't project our own weaknesses onto others by laying blame and anticipating reactions that actually don't exist except in ourselves. And it is not so easy to believe that we really do make our own reality, and we really can be anything we want to be, as long as we have the Will to achieve.

For many people, the miseries in their past, and the

words "Can't" and "No Choice" remain deeply rooted in the mind, - born perhaps from a habit of a lifetime – and I have often wished these words could be deleted from the dictionary, for "Can't" is often another way of saying "I don't want to": and we *always do* have choices – it is just that some are worse than others.

Those who found it too demanding dropped away, but many stayed to finish their courses, which lasted for well over 12 years. However, from my experience I found that, for everyone the involvement had a profound affect on their lives, whether they continued to study or not. And this was not because of Maat, but simply that the subjects taught resonated with the truth.

The study of the Tree of Life became invaluable, for it afforded the opportunity to move slowly from one level of self-awareness to the next, in simple more logical steps than random meditation - yet with visualisation as its' foundation.

Thus, it became the focal point of the journey: leading from the often sadly derided Astrology and Tarot: onto the Qabalah: gradually examining the ten fundamental aspects of self, and taking command of the imagination to share in the beauty of temples, including other worlds right at the heart of ourselves.

Many came through recommendation and others just out of vague interest. Some weren't really sure what to think, even though they were always encouraged to query as much as was needed. However, the most avid cynic must have secretly wanted to believe, or they wouldn't have stayed - even though there were a few rather outlandish things that confronted them at times.

Once, I bought a life size knight that took pride of place in the hall by the Tardis. I was very proud of him, for he fitted with the scenery, and had personal significance for another very dear aspirant who had recently also died of cancer. Bill – 'The Boot' - as he was known, had owned a shoe shop in the Village arcade, and had been a good friend for many years. To me, this knight was quite innocent, but in pursuit of remembrance, I didn't fully appreciate the awesome affect it may have on some people.

The hall was large, chilly, and frequently candle lit, which I suppose added to the atmosphere. Lorraine recently told me that the knight really increased her alarm when she passed it to come back into her beginner's class, only to find the door handle turning before she could open it. Because she herself was quite a sceptic, this left her thinking she would look an utter fool if she said anything to the class, and it was a long time before she realised that others were experiencing the same sort of things, but didn't say anything for fear of ridicule!

Of course, all this wasn't surprising, as we had already discovered that the house was haunted when purchased, and we did have a phantom child living with us then.

Barry, being an excellent medium, had spoken of a young girl watching him from a distance as he worked. Sandy, who looked through the letterbox before I moved in, insisted she saw her running down the stairs, and I also met her rather suddenly one night, when woken by the cold to find her sitting right on top of me. It was really rather a shock, as she was trying to stroke my hair, but her hand kept passing through my face, which seemed to distress her even more than myself!

Later it was discovered there was a young girl called Christine who lived and died there in Victorian times. Being mentally sick, she never left the house, and was looked after by a number of carers until she passed on when very young. It took her a while to realise she was no longer incarnate, and I think she believed that we were just other people that had come to look after her.

She stayed for quite some time, and seemed to particularly enjoy the lessons, often squeezing between people with a chilly embrace.

And then there was Galdoon – a very large elemental – who moved in about a year later, and decided to take permanent residence in one of the rooms created as a woodland temple at the top of the house. The first time I met him he was stomping on my pillow, which was another alarming incident, as he had an outlandish face, and was nearly the size of a miniature toddler.

He made a huge amount of noise, thumping and banging, and when he first arrived he developed an immense fondness for a long school dinner table, which ironically had been sawn down to fit his height. Paul and I used to hear him tramping along it in the night. So much so that one time he made such a noise that Paul thought we had a burglar and insisted on calling the police.

After all these years, it was quite normal for me to experience these things, but to others it must have been more than freaky, I suppose.

So, if you are thinking all this sounds completely crazy, I do appreciate that believing in the reality of the Elemental Kings and their kingdoms is one of the hardest things for many to accept, and I suspect that some never do. I doubt if I would have done in the past, but the imagination of my grandmother and John were excellent tutors in that field, and I often wished I could express their magic in the same way.

From a more logical viewpoint it's easier to explain that all energy is life in one form or another, and as humanity we have found to our cost that, when the elements opt to collide with our worlds, we can only be the losers.

So maybe it was not too prudent to dismiss these elementals for, in the bigger picture of life, we are told by the wise that they are also as much part of our own world as the elements they portray.

Many people see them, and to many people they really exist.

I remember talking animatedly to an elemental once. I had always seen them, but it was the first time I had heard one actually speak to me, although Barry always did. So, being very excited, I had the most remarkable unintelligible conversation, until I realised I was communing with my stomach.

But then again, half the fun is to remain open to being stupid at times, even if we do believe.

32 THE BIGGER PICTURE

"If I have seen further, it was because I stood on the shoulders of giants"
Isaac Newton

It has to be said that although we do all have our own choice in our destiny, much of it may seem pre-ordained by circumstances greater than our present time. When you look back over your life and direction, you may wonder sometimes how much you personally took part in decisions that you perceived to be you own, and how much was pre-destined by Karmic conditions of much larger proportions than just your present existence?

That's how it was for me.

Throughout the long years I had stumbled through my scepticism to the wall of the inconceivable, and opened a gateway that I thought was the final realisation, only to find out that this just led onto another pathway reaching further and further, beyond the worlds of our own imagination, and into the many other worlds of alternative realities.

And I knew then, that to recognise these things was not about refusing to face life: it was about realising there is another side to reality that is equally important. There was so much hidden magic around us: so much beauty: so many things to still discover beyond this earthly plane: and other people, if willing, could be helped to find them too.

Deep humility became a key factor in my understanding, for I was still a simple student tentatively scratching at the roots of enlightenment and, as time progressed, I became more and more certain that I was no more in charge of surrounding events than a child is in charge of its parent when it seeks to take it's hand.

The decisions I made were apparently mine, but I became very aware that these were only manipulating a sequence of time so vast by comparison to my existence that my personal Will had little if anything to do with it. I seemed to be striding through barrier upon barrier of inner revelations and moving determinedly towards a goal that kept changing shape and stepping out of sight in front of me.

Coupled with that I was being given profound information, not just in my thoughts as before, but also in clear words from a male voice, as if in dictation. These communications extended way beyond the limitations of my own mind, and always left me exhausted yet deeply moved by their wisdom.

This was not the same powerful male voice that I had heard when in hospital, although I did hear that too a number of times over the years. However, this was only at moments of great significance to myself, and often when I was too caught up in earthly events to properly listen or interpret important personal guidance.

No, these other communications were coming from a much more advanced source, which I was soon to discover were from the Masters - The Lords of Karma, and The Lords of Peace - who reside on the Inner Planes.

They too are part of our life swarm, but these are truly enlightened souls that had once stood where we are now, and through this experience, their teachings – often in the form of a parable - still remain as meaningful today as they were when given to me then, and no doubt have endured throughout the ages.

These Great Beings were to become vital in my mystical training, as well as that of the more advanced students, and indeed have always been equally vital to the spiritual advancement of humanity.

As time moved on, I became aware that I had also come under the tuition of one specific Great Master - who initially showed himself as a beautiful, dark, and powerful eagle, known by the name of Gor. Thus began a long and deeply intense connection that lasted for many years.

How this came about was both extraordinary and deeply moving, but must remain part of another story. It is enough to say that this connection, and subsequent instruction, became one of the most wonderful and profound experiences of my life.

I must admit that I became more than a little awestruck by these encounters, and immensely daunted by the weight of responsibility that I had attracted upon my shoulders. For nothing was simple anymore, and I realised that quite unintentionally I had founded an organisation that was now moving forward into a much bigger picture, yet with me, as a mere human infant, holding the reigns.

The full reality of this finally dawned on me after I shut the door on the last student of the night at 11.30pm one evening in early July 1997.

It had been a very difficult time, for John had recently died, and I was still suffering the same nightmare of sorrow I had experienced with my father, 10 years before, but this time I didn't shut myself away.

Matt had gone into the throws of unutterable grief, and my heart wept for us all, as I stood with him watching Marilyn tearfully placing a single red rose on John's grave. This once strong and vibrant man had made such an impact on everyone he met – even Simon, who had remained a little aloof from him in his teenage years. No, he would never be forgotten.

But I knew by then that when we love someone so very deeply, they remain rooted in our aura. On death, they are removed, leaving behind a rip that has to have time to heal. Part of that healing for me was to realise that every great love, in life or death, is a gift given that should never be wasted - it has infinite value when nurtured and cherished to support our earthly future.

The session had been long that evening, for I had been teaching the seven phases of death, which had caused much discussion, and had brought me so much closer to the pain of personal loss.

By then, part of the ground floor had been made into a small private flat for myself – courtesy of Ruth's husband David, who also converted the basement. I was very tired, but didn't feel inclined to go to bed, and climbed the stairs to the Sky Temple at the top of the house.

The candles had long since faded, but the room remained aglow with illuminated stars, fixed to the ceiling painted with one stray cloud in an indigo sky. This was an enchanted place at night, for it was as if the area was suspended in space, and I felt I needed something special that evening.

John loved the idea of being out in space, and I felt closer to him there. Lying down on one of the wide side seats used for meditation, I closed my eyes, looked back, and remembered.

"Take up your sword and fight!"

How ironical that I didn't know how significant those words were until I took up the study of The Tree of Life - for the sword is symbolic of the Spiritual Will. And yes, it had taken all of my Will to stay on this path.

I smiled, remembering Lorraine's first life changing experience of subtle forces at work in the temple one evening. She always claimed she was a blank canvass, open to influence, but she wasn't easily diverted from factual evidence. To her, a spade was a spade, and sometimes she was not very tactful in her search for the truth, yet always remained with an open heart and willingness for logical discussion.

After a long intense session, she confided that half way through she had suddenly felt a warm and comforting touch, first on her head and then on the top of her arm.

"For a moment", she laughed, "I really thought I'd finally been 'touched by the hand of God', but then I realised I had a dollop of candlewax on my head and shoulder!"

We all laughed too, but I really think this was a turning point for her, as it was very clear that, from where she was sitting, she was nowhere near any candles at all,. As her passion grew, she reminded me of my past self in many ways, only she was much more of a warrior. Yet, even at that stage neither of us knew that she would subsequently become an indispensable asset to the future - after the closure of Maat.

A motorbike pulled up outside, and left its' engine running for ages. A woman came out from somewhere, and screeched at a guy for another age.

He then told her to "**F............................ off!**" in a long unmelodious note, before revving away at a furious pace. A door slammed loudly. Briefly, a lone dog barked, and then there was quiet again.

"That's the way of the world", I grinned to myself "Everything is so huge to some, and loud and invasive to others, yet we are all so small amongst it all.

I wondered if those people, in their very earthly arena, were aware of others like me, lying there in a star-studded chamber, ruminating about the eternal cycle of life and death, and even now continuing to struggle to make sense of it all. How stupid it all seemed, and how terribly insignificant I felt.

John's untimely death: the heartbreak of my mother's story, as well as all our personal tragedies and grief, were only a minute part of the universal stage, and so unimportant by comparison - yet so huge if looked at from the perception of our own personal worlds.

But there was a much bigger, brighter picture as my father had said. Something that maybe we couldn't quite see because of its' size, but in our minds and hearts we could reach out and touch - for we are part of this and we each have a place in it as surely as night follows day.

Yet how do you explain to those standing in a muddy emotional puddle, that it doesn't matter, because their dark place is intrinsic to The Great Cosmic Plan, and part of the Magical Image of creation?

Does it make it easier to be assured that we are all Divine in our own right: that each of us has an equally important position in a much bigger picture, and every one of us – however insignificant - have special soul functions, soul names and mottos, including a specific karmic role to play?

To me, the Tree of Life was not just a series of circles thought up by dreamers, but a map that covers all life's possible experiences, with origins stemming back to the time of Abraham.

It explained so many things, and answered so many questions.

I wanted to stand on mountains and shout that there

was a way that could help, if we wanted. A way that encompassed both scientific and spiritual worlds: provided credible explanations of the more hidden aspects written in our holy books: pointed to other dimensions in other galaxies, and examined the 10 faces of the Cosmos; of our Creator; the Angelic host; the prophets; nature; and finally ourselves.

And if we studied this Tree carefully, it would show us how all these things were designed to fit together. So why wasn't it better known?

I shifted uneasily, for I was fast getting beyond myself in frustration and upset. In my stricken mood, I seriously wondered why I had chosen such a terribly lonely and difficult task, for there had been so many long phases of inadequacy and inner desperation. I didn't have any earthly mentors and, as time progressed, was becoming more and more reliant on information coming from other realms.

I went over to the stereo, and switched on the radio, hoping it would calm me and turn my mind to other things. A record played. It was John Lennon's "Imagine". The same song that had affected me so greatly, whilst filled with anticipation during the Rainbow days. How strange it should be playing just now. But then again, nothing is coincidental, is it?

My heart ached, and I sat down holding my head in my hands, thinking of my mother, still alone in her world: Dale and Keith in theirs: even my sons, neglected as they had been on this eternal journey that had given up so many secrets, but still threatened to never end. All these years, and I hadn't told my brothers anything, or attempted to write my mother's story. Why not? What was I frightened of? I didn't know, but somehow it wasn't yet the time.

I really wanted to cry, but again I couldn't. It had sort of dried up inside me, and I was unable to find a way to release the grief. I remembered the words my mother had spoken on that anguished day after the death of my father. How terrible it must have been for her to suffer that sort of pain for all those years.

"So is this what it's all about?" I wondered. "Here I am, surrounded by wonderful friends and the support and protection of all those on the astral and Inner Planes, but nevertheless so terribly alone in my own personal inadequacy" – because that's the way it is when we walk onto the road that flashes with the brilliance of wondrous anticipation, without true knowledge of real enlightenment.

And I suppose it was at that moment, that I realised I didn't actually have to fight anymore, and maybe now could finally let go the reins, for It suddenly became absolutely clear that, wherever I found myself on that day, it had only been through the help of so many great teachers along the way.

My wonderful, dear, dear, grandmother and her unwavering belief in "Make Believe" who had lit a spark that eventually led me to this vital doorway of understanding. My so special mother, and her desperate fight with reality, whose haunting cry had pulled me out of my dream world, into a quest that would eventually lead to my destiny: and my father, my beloved father, who in his amazing tolerance taught me so much about humility and acceptance of a more objective viewpoint.

There were others too: my brothers, my children: the loves of my life, my dear loyal friends – yet nevertheless very ordinary people, who would never know what they had done to irrevocably affect my learning and life - those, too many to mention, who deserved immense gratitude.

And not least, I had been lucky enough to be in touch with these teachers of the inner worlds; those who showed me the wonder of imagination, and the incredible strength of the subconscious – **guides, doorkeepers, guardians and finally the Masters** - Forces of almost unimaginable power and wisdom beyond our earthly vision. They have so much to teach, and in fact had been saying things for time immemorial, to anyone who would listen long enough to transmit their messages.

How very foolish I had been to think that I was ever alone. I was totally supported in every way, and my job: my work: my quest – was almost done, but there was still just a little more to do.

Slowly I got up and made my way downstairs, briefly touching the knight on his arm as I passed by.

"Goodnight, Bill," I whispered, "Goodnight, old friend".

****

In December 1999, my mother died, and I felt glad that maybe she would finally find some peace.

For a number of years after those fateful days in 1987, she had lived alone in the family house. However, in spite of the fact that she had finally been able to tell her story, she had reverted back to the familiar erratic and volatile world she had been obliged to create for herself – a place of contrived safety, maybe?

Dale always believed Mum would be better in a home, but Keith and myself felt strongly that if she was taken off medication and given a chance, she may have been able to live a more fulfilling life. Nevertheless, we were sadly mistaken for it was all too late and, to my utmost regret, she never mentally recovered.

In the time that followed, she had no desire for anyone to live with her, and really made it quite impossible for anyone to do so. Later, carers looked after her for a while, but in the end she spent her last few years in a home, and looking back, I really believe that Dale was right, for these were probably the happiest days of her life.

After our mother's death, Joan at last confirmed everything about the past, and I was indeed grateful for that. She told me my Grandfather and Doris had forbidden her to speak about it, because "…it would hurt Nora". So she didn't - evading my questions when asked. I couldn't criticise, for she was only 6 years old when it all happened, and must have believed what they told her.

In 2001 Campbell Road was sold and if it were ever possible to say that a house could be the love of a life, I would choose that one. A very special memorial garden had been built for John in the front, and for me that is where he will always remain. However, it was not until November 2005, when the last groups finished, that Maat finally closed.

2 weeks later, I collapsed.

So that was it. My fathers' wisdom had stood the test of time, for there are indeed only two pathways that we can follow in search for a solution to a difficult problem - the chance to change things or the chance to stand still and accept them. I couldn't accept it, so I tried to change it. Whether I was successful or not really doesn't matter, for through it all I learned so much.

You know, anyone can follow the so-called "irrational" road I took, if they seriously wish to do so. It is not so strange, for it is just the story of the 2 sides of life, and the sacred magical reality of our own Destiny and Divinity.

However, it is not for the fantasists, floaters, or the slight of heart. It is not for those who wish to play at New Age reverie: nor for those who think they can make a quick buck or raise themselves as Gods. It is for the committed aspirant who is prepared to be challenged every step of the way.

Early in childhood, my godmother Sheila told me that life is about spiritual growth. It is not about achieving stardom, or even recognition in earthly terms. If credit comes, it is a bonus, but not the purpose of our efforts. For me, she was right, for the rewards of this mystical study are far more valuable than that, and can be likened to re-discovering a hidden Treasure house of lost jewels that had long since been forgotten - except in my dreams.

AFTER

"Show me a sane man and I will cure him for you."
Carl Jung

After her funeral, it was a long 9 years, before I finally said goodbye to my mother, and it is probably only now that it seems right to tell her story.

When Maat closed, I had become ill for a long time, and although we never fell out, I certainly lost contact with my brothers after Mum died. However, due to Matt's loyal and very caring nature, I was eventually reunited with them through him, and, together with both my sons, we scattered her ashes in a quiet and beautiful place, overlooking the sea.

I speak to Dale and Keith regularly these days. I find great joy in their company, and will make sure we will not lose touch again. There were many valuable years missed, but maybe not altogether lost. Perhaps they will disagree with my version of our childhood events, but I can honestly say that I have written this book as close as I can to the eye of truth.

However I am well aware that, although we may sincerely believe in the accuracy of our own recollections, there must be certain discrepancies, for memories hang very much on the background, temperament and the personal reactions of each individual.

The three of us only talked very briefly about our background before starting this book, and already there are some incidents that Dale doesn't remember, yet Keith tells me he recalls things that I never thought he knew.

Perhaps some things have been forgotten, or blanked from the mind, and other events could have appeared more intense than they actually were. It's true that the consciousness will reject what is too hurtful to see; but the mind can also exaggerate to explain the inner pain. So all I can deduce from that is we "only see what we want to see" as Gran always said.

However, for me, some questions still remain, and for our mother's sake shouldn't be forgotten because it may be unpleasant to remember. Was she actually mentally ill, or was her personality deeply fragmented, firstly through not being allowed to express her childhood grief, and secondly through the drugs and treatments she further received?

It's too late now to change the result of what happened to her, but it's surely not too late to look at the treatments of mental health from a different and possibly more imaginative angle?

I am not "officially" qualified to deal with this, but my experience in trying to unravel the subject must extend further than learning by degree. I wonder why experience doesn't command more respect - for without it, surely a piece of paper has little to do with the reality of "hands on" involvement?

There is an increase in mental illness in 2014. It is getting worse, and teenage suicide is also on the increase. Why is this? Could it be that we have got lost somewhere in the middle of our fear of reprisal and political correctness, which restricts healthy freedom to make mistakes, and puts us in danger of suffocating the natural growth of enquiring minds?

In my time there was a great deal of hope and a lot of faith. We were not always perfectly safe, but we gained confidence in learning how to deal with danger ourselves, rather than by enforced regulation. Belief and trust was easier to sustain then. Now, in this technological age, the heart of humanity seems to be struggling against the influx of negative information that social media and the Internet have brought to our door – celebrity idolism, encouragement of greed, cyber bullying, and coverage of eternal wars, to name but a few.

This overall atmosphere of anticipated terrorism and adversity must surely cultivate a feeling of hopelessness in the young? So maybe it is not so much about wanting to die, but finding living so very hard these days?

I wonder why we can't all at least *try* to find something we can agree with in each other, or is it *really* going to take a marauding comet or the loss of the moon to finally unite us?

We may have opposing opinions, but does that make any of us really wrong? Maybe all of us are right in our own way, but just sitting at opposite ends of the one Great Picture of life?

So while we are being told that our overall mental health is stumbling in this enlightened age, are we actually moving forward and finding ourselves introduced to anything really new?

I recently heard a programme, supposed to be very advanced in new understanding. These were eminent people, with notable degrees. And yet a young psychiatrist clearly voiced the opinion that,

"Hearing voices: seeing things that are not there, and other such weird beliefs, have no place in reality"

Well now, I feel it's imperative to seriously challenge this thinking – at least for my own sake, if not for my mother's.

I have heard voices, and seen things that others can't, and if "proof" is the requirement to say that they exist, then what actual "proof" is there to say they don't? Most scientists will confirm that "scientific proof" is often gleaned only from experiments that fit the theory.

I don't take drugs, and if I am indeed "mentally challenged", as the new word for "deluded" - amongst other things – suggests, then I have to say I am quite proud of it, for without my belief to sustain me, I doubt if people would have stayed in my classes, and I wouldn't have been able to hold things together throughout all these years.

Of course there is *distorted* thought, but there is also *different* thought, and who in the world is completely sane, or really qualified to know the difference?

What worries me greatly is that I don't see much real change or progress in the treatments of mental heath today, as compared to my mother's time.

In an interview as late as 2013, Frank Bruno said the medication he was given during his breakdown, made him like a zombie, which sounds a very familiar note from the past. And a recent discovery of TMS – firing magnetic pulses into the brain - seems no different to me than the dreadful electrical treatments of my mother's time.

There's considerable argument about cannabis, and how it is believed by some to distort the mind, yet it is apparently safe enough to be prescribed for sufferers of multiple sclerosis today.   Amazingly, my mother was actually treated with hallucinogens like LSD, and later Largatil – a medication, whose side effects are now known to fragment the personality.   These were recognised as approved treatments then – so where's the logic in being blinded to other unusual, but much safer, ideas now?

Doesn't this just show that after all this time, the call of yesterday still applies today - and maybe it would be useful to take a look in another direction? This is not about negating what is already there, but perhaps not excluding other more lateral viewpoints that could be useful if fully investigated?

There seems to have been progress in the active use of psychology, but even there, a wide diversion of opinion could hamper progress?

The father of psychoanalysis, Sigmund Freud is best known for his tendency to trace nearly all psychological problems back to sexual issues. He obviously understood the subconscious, but it's difficult for me to appreciate his teachings fully because I feel that my mother fell foul of the medical profession's tunnel vision in their determined adherence to his beliefs.

From my understanding Freud's ideas didn't encourage doctors to pursue a fuller examination of the past, but I am not sure I can think objectively about this without being subconsciously biased. It is true that with progress ideas move one, yet also some may have been too easily overlooked?

Newton, Einstein and Jung, advocated the psychological value of Astrology, and also studied the Tree of Life, so surely they knew what they were talking about - especially as Jung was a much respected and eminent psychiatrist?

It still seems to me, that our education is such that the vital things are overlooked, or dismissed or feared because they don't belong to the accepted scale of credibility. Yet, through this misunderstanding, there could be so much unnecessary suffering and pain, either brought about by the judgements of others, or self-inflicted through lack of true knowledge of ourselves.

I may be an old woman, but I haven't lost my

sensibilities. Whichever way I look, it brings me back to the desperate need for better, more lateral thinking in our education, and particularly in schools. For what is the use of our literacy or maths, if we don't know the very fundamentals of living?

Schooling can do so much to benefit lives, and maybe bring back a little more understanding of where we stand in the bigger picture of life. After all, what could be more exciting for a child, but to be shown how to learn about themselves, their classmates, and their world?

Those who have seriously studied astrology, know that it is not really a forecasting, but more of an analytical machine. It is mathematically based, and linguistic skills are essential in interpretation. The first astronomers were also astrologers, and the Tree of Life is also just one simple design that can be used to encompass many other subjects we require for a good overall education.

There were so many coincidences, and wonders that are too readily still dismissed without scrutiny, and yet surely, if we learned to recognise such things as they passed us by, we would have a far better chance of using these forces to benefit our lives? We just need to be educated to learn how to see and tap them.

Shakespeare called the world a stage, with us as mere players in the act of life. In the same way, it is also true that we are all – adult or child - in a massive schoolroom, and taking exams in life. Some are good at it, others are not, and others just beginning on their course of study. If we understood that, maybe there would be more tolerance of our mistakes, because we'd more easily accept that we are all learning together?

Anyway, all this is again from my own perspective, but I am glad many have shared the same views.

During the 25 years of Maat's existence, well over 6,000 people came through the doors, entirely through recommendation, and I am pleased that the teachings will now continue into the daily lives of individuals, and particularly those who have gone on to start their own groups in line with their own particular skills.

Some have written books, and made quite an impact in the media world, and others have silently followed their own dreams far beyond the realms of everyday life. If I have had an influence upon them, I am privileged, for it's very clear that these people have always been masters of their own destiny, and whether they make the history books or not, they are worthy inheritors of whatever "success" means to them.

Maat made way for the founding of The Order of The White Lion (OWL) in 2002, and I opened a website, with the help of Drew - a brilliant IT merchant and another dedicated aspirant, whose loyalty and expertise is still invaluable to us today. Shortly after that, Owl and Isis Workshops began, and Lorraine stepped forward to take the helm.

From my experience, anything of value comes from people working together, with no one individual holding themselves up as superior to any other. There are leaders, but it is the job of those who come after to extend, adapt, and overtake the information already gained.

In these mystical realms, I have constantly come across people prepared to jog along, – holding themselves up as Gods – but not prepared to risk delving further into the unseen worlds. However, there are other people programmed to push beyond the boundaries, extending and developing on what has gone before. These people form their own very personal connections with the great teachers of the Inner Planes in order to become advocates for progress - and Lorraine is one of them.

Over the years, I watched her as she struggled, fought and learned in her own indomitable way. Hers was not a gentle road, for being a catalyst by nature she queries everything, and continuously challenges the automatic structure of events. Nevertheless, this dedication has served to make her master of her own fate and she has become an exceptional tutor.

Over the last few years she has taken all Maat teachings and done an excellent job in reconstructing, developing, simplifying and consolidating everything, to formulate a complete series of beautifully illustrated workbooks that take the student slowly on a step-by-step journey through the Tree of Life, in a simple, logical, but enchanting way. For this massive effort, I am both grateful and very proud.

I am 73 years old now, and when I look back I can see many things that I could have done better. In fact, when feeling quite clever in my discoveries, it was soon made obvious I was actually more of an ass with good intentions.

In some ways this book could be called "The Sins of the Fathers" for certainly the events of the past were visited upon us all. So I suppose the memory belongs to the whole family - including this fragment of history bequeathed to our children.

Not least, it is written for my brothers who, like myself, were so deeply involved and responsive to the shadow of events that took place in our younger days. We followed different paths, with different outlooks, for different reasons, yet each of us was greatly affected by the same reality in the beginning – the strange and "unreal" worlds of the mentally ill.

I believe I have found some of "the answer" that I set out to find all those years ago, but nevertheless, too late for my mother. To me, she was seriously let down by the system, and for reasons given, I am not too sure she would fare much better today.

It is obvious that I reacted to my mother as she had reacted to hers. Was I obsessed? Yes. Was I arrogant to think I could make a difference? Probably. Yet, maybe both those things ensured momentum to try to clear a little bit of the karmic debris along the path?

I wish that I could have done more to ease her burden, and I am sorry that my preoccupation led to the neglect of my boys - at least in the sense of them not having the comfort of a more "normal" mother. But then, they are born of our family stock, so I was always going to be very proud of what they would become, and grateful for their strength and continued support in my latter years - which I am not too sure I really deserve.

I live with Matt on the Isle of Wight now, who looks after me wonderfully. We laugh a lot, and are very content in each other's company. A neighbour's cat sits in the garden everyday, musing in sun or rain, and assorted birds nest in the hedge, but the crows have moved up the road to Rookley these days.

It is also greatly comforting to share times with Simon as much as possible, even though he lives some distance away. He is such a gentle wise old soul, and his sound advice is very reassuring as time moves on.

Although I don't see much of Ian now, I will always remember the immense help he gave me in forming a solid base for Maat. He is owed a great deal for his effort and vision, and I'm very grateful for that. Happily dear Jenny remains regularly in touch, and, I often hear from Paul too who is still composing his music and songs in Ireland now.

As for my special loyal friend Sandy, she travels over here quite often. Together, we are still rather like 'Hinge and Bracket', with me more than a little decrepit as we wander around, spending long slow times by the sea, wining and dining, and laughing at the old days and the crazy situations we found ourselves in. Sometimes we discuss the strange recognition, affinity, and upsurge of memories that she and my mother both had when they met. There was obviously a reason, and we have our own ideas about that.

This has been a long and eventful tale, but hopefully will resonate with curious minds and help to explain how, often unconsciously governed by our Will, we all follow a definitive path in life without even realising we are doing so.

Perhaps it also illustrates, how many great teachers are lined up to help each of us, in any direction we choose to take - parents, children, siblings, friends and enemies, students, spiritual tutors, guides on many levels, and yes indeed even The Masters – if we can be bothered to recognise them and take note of the clues and lessons they leave behind.

We all travel on our own road, and follow our own star to our own destiny. How much we can control this and appreciate where we are going is down to our own interpretation, observation, and recognition of the obvious incidents that are placed before us - and there always will be signposts for those who care to look.

I suppose it could be argued that the earth plane is the place where we take the life exam that destiny has set us for this incarnation?

And maybe part of this is to understand the importance of us all being equivalent in what we do, for surely it is about us all linking together at our own level in this great work of creation - and at whatever level we are now, it is pre-designed to make us *all* equally essential to the Great Cosmic Plan?

There *is* a reality in the unseen – vital and dynamic in its power – but I have learned that firstly we have to see the signs, study the language, and appreciate that everything is not necessarily the way it may seem.

I have lived an eventful life of wonder and joy, and indeed felt a great deal of pain. But above all, and through it all, I have discovered that even as the world changes, so our own worlds will always remain a reflection of our own design.

We are Divine Sparks: part of the life swarm of humanity. We are personalities, souls and spirits. We have potential to be gods. We are sovereigns in our own kingdoms, and we all have a tale to tell.

So this is just one story – my dear mother's and mine.

It was for this I was born, and have lived.

THE DREAM

"Reality is merely an illusion, albeit a very persistent one."
Albert Einstein

One day I dreamed a dream that took me into a world of time they called "reality".

A star came and walked with me. It said its' name was Destiny and Fate: and when I strayed from my soul chosen path, Fate followed, nudging me back to the crossroads where Destiny waited, and together we continued on our way.

In my dream I watched, and saw a child's view of a crisis lead on to the foot of a Cosmic Mirror, where images of other worlds could only be seen by reflection: and they called these worlds "illusion".

But I knew they were there, because I could see the orchestra, and hear the music, and saw that their complex variety was as breathtaking and exquisite as snowflakes adrift in the sky.

And I dreamt that others could see this splendour too, if they tried.

So, have you ever looked up at a canopy of stars and wished you could fly free with the wind, or dream a beautiful story that never ends?

Well, this is your day, and you are living your dream right now - for you are born into your kingdom, with you as the Sovereign.

Close your eyes, and open your mind; and if you don't like what you see, you can change it - if you want to.

But if it's fear that besieges you, then - you have the Will - stand firm and confront it with courage. Reclaim your crown from its' cheating head, for this fervent imposter has no place in the cosmic dream.

That is how we find our freedom and learn to fly.

And when your day is done, you will see you have inscribed your personal epitaph through your own actions and desire – so take care that what you write is how you wish to be remembered.

In my dream I saw and heard strange things; went to enchanted places beyond this human existence, and through it all I laughed with joy, yet cried a river.

And it was on this day I learned, that without the vision there can be no dreams, and without the risks there can be no miracles.

APPENDIX

* The Qabalah and The Tree of Life

To study the Qabalah is to examine life on every level – from the physical to the higher spiritual creation – and this is just one aspect of it, for it also encompasses a spectrum of infinite possibilities, including the idea of other worlds, the magical power of number, language, and universal concepts that move us closer to understanding of our origins and destiny.

There are many disagreements about the subject, even down to the spelling of the name. It is better known as Kabbalah or Cabala, but the word Qabalah has been introduced by those studying it in the west. Most believe that it is of Jewish origin, for it has been known as the 'Mystical interpretation of the Old Testament' and those who study it, say it gives many explanations of biblical statements and apparent contradictions that have sometimes confused understanding.

There are also many arguments as to what is or is not the Qabalah, and indeed the right ways of accessing it. However, The Tree of Life is so versatile, it seems to encompass all things for all people, and therein lies its infinite worth - for whether we are of strong religious persuasion or not; a dreamer, pragmatist, or simply just a querent, it acknowledges such variety of opinion, yet opens doorways of new perception that help us find out where we come from, what we believe in, and above all the reasons why we do so.

Nevertheless, the subject is not a religion, but more a philosophy of a way of life, and it arguably fulfils our need for both magic and realism, yet confronts our sceptical selves and patiently walks us through the shadows of our own disbelief.

Its value lies in the use of The Tree of life as a profound psychological 'tool', and its study can be likened to taking a Degree in Life.

**Guides of the Human Life swarm.

Disincarnate beings reside on the levels beyond our earth plane. These are our helpers and mentors on other planes and, according to the position they are placed, work with us at different levels of understanding.

Whoever we are, we all have our own spiritual connections with various disincarnate friends, helpers and teachers on other planes, who can also aid us immensely in life.

Personal Guides reside in what is often known as the "Local Astral" plane. It is far less dense than the physical world, and it is believed that this is where we go directly after we die. Most "beings" on this plane can be classified as very like ourselves, but perhaps with a slightly more objective view than we are able to perceive.

Every individual on the earth plane has a "Personal Guide" from the Astral Plane, who stays with them throughout their incarnate life, and is there to help guide them through the hazards of everyday living.

Doorkeepers. Every person also has a Doorkeeper with them throughout life, although only at specific times. They too reside on the "Astral Plane", but are more specialised than personal guides. Clairvoyants often see them as warriors, and their function is to protect our subconscious mind.

When doing any form of spiritual work we open up to emotional experiences beyond the physical plane. The Doorkeeper's job is to open the "door" to our mind; to protect us from unwanted interference while we work; and close it after we have finished. This allows easy return to our earthly life, and prevents unnecessary loss of energy.

Both our Personal Guides and Doorkeepers are totally dedicated to our personal welfare.

Visiting Guides. These guides are part of what is known as the "Upper Astral" worlds, and are associated with the logical and creative sides of ourselves. These worlds are on a higher plane, and are more advanced and ethereal.

Sometimes, when a person becomes increasingly committed to an intellectual activity or artistic objective, certain Guides from the respective worlds will move in to aid them in their endeavour.They are called "Visiting" or "Temporary" Guides, as they only stay as long as the person is concentrating on that activity. When the learning phase is over, they will pass on to aid someone else.

Soul Guides. These Guides are far more advanced than previous guides, and not interested in personality issues. They no longer need to incarnate, and are involved with the development of the Soul. They are known as the "Lesser Masters".

Each of us has a Soul Guide. They are the mediating force between the person we know as "Me" in our everyday life (the personality), and the Soul that we are, in the much higher sense.

The Soul Guide is interested in developing moral values, and it is their job to help us make the transition from the self-centred, emotionally reactive individual, to the "soul conscious" dedicated aspirant on the road to enlightenment.

The Masters – Inner Plane Adepti

At this level the Guides are extremely ethereal, exceptionally highly advanced, and can be looked upon as the Hierarchy of Humanity.

These Sacred Guides – Lords of Karma and Lords of Peace - are the "Sages" of the Inner Worlds, who have long since become "Adepts" of the lower levels, and have no further need for incarnation on the physical plane.

They are sometimes known as The Brotherhood, or the Ascended Masters, and indeed, they have earned the right to ascend to the highest levels of existence, but have chosen to remain in their present position in order to support and aid those who are following in their footsteps.

Their concentration is not on individuals, but the soul development of the whole of humanity.

The Lords of Karma are the Overseers and Assessors of Human Conscience, and their interest is in the Fiery Sword of Truth. The Law of Cause and Effect applies across all levels of the Universe, and it is their job to evaluate and reconcile individual, family, national, and international Karmic conditions in order to balance the Cosmic Scales of Justice.

The Lords of Peace are Teachers and Mentors of human values, and their interest is in the Vision of a perfected species that will develop and evolve in natural alignment with the overall Cosmic Plan. Their job is to counsel and help raise human consciousness, in preparation for the spiritual journey into the upper worlds.

These beings are the Masters of the Jigsaw of Life. Their job is infinite, and far beyond our own comprehension, for they have a total view of all things that make up the light and shade of our fragile species.

Although the Masters of the Inner Planes are only interested in the evolution of the whole of humanity, they do, on rare occasions, take on the instructive role of teachers and advisors of certain individuals whose intense dedication and spiritual involvement shows signs of usefulness to the advancement of the species.

These people will often find themselves "driven" for no apparent reason, and the more they live with an open heart and passionate spirit, the more "the light" in the crown centre shines - almost like a candle in the dark - which may eventually catch the attention of the hierarchy.

And if this happens - and only if the disciple is prepared to completely commit to the Call of the Masters - they will be deeply tested, honed, and trained to become earthly Spiritual Advisors, whose job it is to enhance the awareness of the "awakening" minds of their peers.

This is how true Spiritual Schools begin, and continue to progress only with the permission and specific guidance of the Great Masters involved.

Thus humanity proceeds on its long journey back to the source of creation.

Note

More detailed information about the Tree of Life, including Guides, Doorkeepers and Masters, can be found at www.orderofthewhitelion.com

and www.isisqabalahtuition.com

Owl and Isis Workbooks

"I, like many others who studied at the School of Maat, experienced a strong compulsion to pass on all that I had learnt once my training was complete.

On the Tree of Life, the message of the Hierophant (spiritual teacher) relates to the lack of purpose in spiritual work unless it is put to practical use. Therefore, to the best of my ability, I have done this in the form of the Tree of Life Workbooks. The workbooks are my way of giving something back in exchange for the inspirational guidance I received under the tuition of Jenni Shell, and the direction of those they call the Masters.

I thank everyone who has played a part in my life. It has been those experiences - particularly the dramas - that has helped me in my quest to fulfill my commitment, and hopefully others can now experience for themselves the wonder and magic of the Tree of Life."

Lorraine Morgan

Tree of Life workbooks in the series

Copyright Jenni Shell and Lorraine Morgan

The following workbooks are step by step guides, designed for beginners to aid the student on their journey of self discovery exploring the Qabalistic Tree of Life.

As in all things, a good place to start is at the beginning and the sephirah of the Earth Plane:

Malkuth - The Kingdom
When studying the Qabalah we often start off at the bottom of the Tree of Life, and begin by familiarising ourselves with the sephirah of the Earth Plane, known as The Kingdom. The Hebrew name for this sephirah is Malkuth. Malkuth represents the physical plane - the world we live in, and the way we handle the energy of the material world. We would look to the Temple of Malkuth to help us find answers if we are having problems keeping ourselves grounded; experiencing challenging issues around money, or if we want to find solace and peace to enable us to re-coup lost energy.

Yesod - The Foundation

The temple of Yesod is a beautiful sea temple. This sephirah focuses on the power of our subconscious; our emotional foundation and emotional stability. Yesod also links us to the Astral Worlds and Spirit Guides. We would look to the Temple of Yesod for help with the responsive process; handling emotional reactions; connecting with our Personal guides, and accessing past life information.

Hod - Splendour of the Mind

The sephirah Hod focuses on our Attitude and the power of Thought. Here we explore the Tunnel of the Mind and become more consciously aware of the sort of images we build in our mind. We would look to the Ice temple of Hod to help us to examine our attitude, and change any images that may be negative to our growth. Hod also helps us to build positive imagery eg. Magical Images; to form commitments, and to find the real truth of our thoughts.

Netzach - Victory over Feelings

The teachings of Netzach help us to gain Victory over our Feelings and lift ourselves out of the restrictions of the personality, helping us to raise to the level of the soul - the Sephirah Tiphareth. Netzach acts as a springboard to the upper part of the Tree, but first we have to become aware of how we really feel, and explore our attitude towards relationships - including the relationship we have with Self. Netzach helps us to discover the true nature of who we really are, the magic that lies hidden within just waiting to be brought to life. We would look to the Emerald temple of Netzach for creative inspiration; to help us deal with polarity and relationship issues, and to connect with the magical energy of the rawness of nature.

Tiphareth - Devotion to the Great Work

The sephirah Tiphareth takes us into the realms of the Soul where we get the opportunity to connect and commune with the soul and higher more evolved guides. The virtue of Tiphareth is Devotion to the Great Work and it is important for us to remember that if we wish to pursue spiritual work and be of service in some way to others we must be prepared to work on ourselves, and help our Self rise above the level of the personality when times are challenging. Tiphareth helps us to heal ourselves so we may remain balanced and in harmony no matter what is happening in our everyday lives.

Geburah - Vision of Power

In Geburah we become aware of mightier forces and begin to understand the role of the Soul, and the purpose of Karma. The challenges we face in this life are linked to our past lives. Geburah helps to expose traits within our personality that bind us to the continuous cycle of birth, death and rebirth, and reveals the links we share with others.

It is in Geburah that we experience the Will of the Soul.

Chesed – Mercy

Chesed is where the journey really begins. **Part One** of Chesed takes us in Search of the Truth. Here we explore the Bigger Picture and attempt to strengthen our connection with the Teachers of Humanity - evolved Masters who can teach us how to walk in Time with the natural order of the Universe thus drawing us nearer to finding peace for the soul.

In **Workbook Two** we learn about the Evolution of Flame and the first wave of creation. This workbook raises our awareness of the role the angels and archangels play in the bigger picture, and how they can help us on our journey to enlightenment. In the Temple of Chesed we may catch a glimpse of the part we play in the grand scheme of Life, and find out how we too may be of service to others - just as the Masters, who have walked this journey before us, have been in service to us.

Binah – Understanding

Binah represents the Womb of Creation and Mother of Form.

In this sephirah, at the top of the black pillar of Form, we explore the Principles of Sound and learn how to Silence the Conscious Mind to hear the call of the Spiritual Mother who watches over her children.

Binah is Aima - the bright, fertile Mother of Creation and Ama - the dark, sterile Mother of the Underworld.

It is in Binah that we examine the roots of our Faith and look deeper into the Four Worlds and extended Tree of Life.

Chokmah Soul Functions

In Chokmah we explore the force of our Creative Power and decide how we can be of Service to Humanity. This

Workbook is an Introduction to Soul Functions and can be used in conjunction with the Chokmah Workbooks. Most people are unaware of their Soul Functions or how to perform them in everyday life. To realise our full potential we need to know how to direct our creative power. The Soul Function Workbook explains in more detail what the functions mean and how to recognise them.

Chokmah - Wisdom
Chokmah is the sephirah of Freedom and Spiritual Truths. It is the sephirah that aligns with the Will of the Spirit and Spiritual Direction. In this region of the Tree of Life the aim is to contact our creative power, and bring it down to earth.

In **Chokmah Workbook One** we explore how we use the senses and how we can further stimulate and balance the two hemispheres of the brain to spark the sixth sense (intuition) and third eye into action.

Chokmah is also the sephirah of Wisdom. In **Chokmah Workbook Two** the emphasis is on Divine Wisdom and looking at ways to enter inner worlds of existence. This helps us to develop our psychic ability, and gain insights pertaining to the destiny and spiritual direction of the whole of humanity.

Kether - the Crown
Situated at the top of the Tree of Life on the middle pillar of equilibrium, Kether represents Spiritual Perfection. At this level we are dealing with the intangible. Therefore, as with all the previous sephiroth in this series of workbooks, the approach to Kether is a practical one. In this workbook we attempt to see through the veil of our earthly perceptions. We explore the existence of other dimensions and try to connect with more advanced energies, and - by using an Inner Spirit Meditation - enter the dwelling place of our spirit.

www.orderofthewhitelion.com
www.isisqabalahtuition.com

ABOUT THE AUTHOR

When Jenni Shell was very young her mother was diagnosed with schizophrenia, which left a deep and lasting impact on the whole family.

Trying to understand her mother's suffering, Jenni began to discover spiritual meaning in many so-called 'delusional' realities and synchronicities, which seemed to contradict her traditional upbringing. Hence, she spent a life-long search in an attempt to reconcile reason, practicalities and the soul's cosmic way of communication, which led her into teaching what she had learnt to others.

In 1981 Jenni founded *Maat* – a Mystery and later Qabalah school - designed to inspire individuals to encompass life as personality, soul and spirit, beyond any rigid perspective. Well over 6,000 people from all walks of life attended and have had the chance to work closely with this powerful, down to earth and modest teacher.

Despite her exposure to the public, Jenni has not sought a great deal of public attention. *Worlds Apart* shows why. Her whole life's focus - initially triggered by family trauma – has always remained in exploring the fine line between what can be misunderstood as mental illness on the one hand, and the urgent language of spiritual impressions on the other.

The need to understand the vital forces of the psyche and adjust one's life practically in order to grow as a human being, has always been central to her life and teachings.

Made in the USA
Charleston, SC
23 November 2014